I0138659

Kings, Queens and the Sordid In-between

Published by Brolga Publishing Pty Ltd
ABN 46 063 962 443
PO Box 12544
A'Beckett St
Melbourne, VIC, 8006
Australia

email: markzocchi@brolgapublishing.com.au

All rights reserved. No part of this publication may be reproduced,
stored in a retrieval system or transmitted in any form or by any
means electronic, mechanical, photocopying, recording or otherwise
without prior permission from the publisher.

Copyright © 2016 Stefan Raicu
National Library of Australia
Cataloguing-in-Publication data

      Raicu, Stefan, author.
      Kings, queens and the sordid in-between : an irreverent perspective /
      Stefan Raicu.
      ISBN: 9781925367591 (paperback)
      Subjects: Royal house--Anecdotes.
      Kings and rulers--Anecdotes.
      Dewey Number: 929.7

Printed in Australia
Cover design by Chameleon Design
Typesetting by Elly Cridland

BE PUBLISHED

Publish through a successful publisher. National distribution, Macmillan
& International distribution to the United Kingdom, North America.
Sales Representation to South East Asia
Email: markzocchi@brolgapublishing.com.au

KINGS, QUEENS AND THE SORDID IN-BETWEEN

An Irreverent Perspective

Stefan Raicu

Contents

Disclaimer

The assertions, jokes, satire and (at times absurd) humour contained in this book are presumed to be taken as amusement only and are not, in any way, intended to upset, insult, affront or offend any individual or group of people irrespective of age, gender, race, colour, nationality, religious faith, mental or physical disability, political orientation or sexual preference.

Introduction

The spur that incited me to put together this book was the famous "misogyny speech" of 9 October 2012 delivered in the Federal Parliament by the then Australian Prime Minister, Ms. Julia Gillard.

I should clarify from the outset that my impulse for kicking off this book was not any admiration for what the former PM had to say on that day.

As a very brief background, on that particular occasion Ms. Gillard attacked the then Opposition Leader, Mr Tony Abbott, accusing him of being "every day in every way" sexist and misogynist.

While many acclaimed Ms. Gillard's speech, believing that she had presented sound and compelling arguments on the topics of sexism and misogyny, my reason for not applauding it is that the speech was in effect, as far as I could see, just a political stunt that suited her and her government's agenda at that particular point in time.

The speech was delivered as a counterattack to the Opposition Leader's attempt to have Mr Peter Slipper – one of Ms. Gillard's allies – removed as Speaker of the House of Representatives over a series of obscene text messages that he, Mr Slipper, had sent to an aide.

Some of the tasteless remarks texted by Mr Slipper had been directed at a female Opposition frontbencher who had dared to criticise him.

Common sense tells me that, even if Ms. Gillard's misogyny speech had contained some substance, it completely lacked credibility for the simple reason that, when delivering it, she was protecting and defending her cohort Speaker who, clearly, was guilty of the very same offence she was accusing the Opposition Leader of!

Her speech, however, achieved at least two main things: it brought the topic into public debate, and even prompted the national dictionary to re-evaluate its definition of misogyny.

And on a personal level, it prompted me to think a bit more deeply about what misogyny is.

I'm a migrant from Romania. When I first arrived in this country, my English vocabulary wasn't too vast. It actually consisted of … about two words and 'misogyny' wasn't one of them.

The words were actually 'yes' and 'beer'. Over the years, my vocabulary has developed a little, but I still have difficulty understanding the term misogyny.

It's maybe because I don't really believe that misogyny is an attitude common to "men wearing blue ties", nor to blokes in general. For those unfamiliar with Australian politics, I will add that "men wearing blue ties" was another much publicised expression made up by Ms Julia Gillard, when referring to the then male Opposition Leader, who later succeeded her as Prime Minister. Among his many other flaws as perceived by

Ms Gillard, the poor chap was in the habit of wearing a blue tie! That's sheer disrespect towards women!

Anyway, leaving Mr Abbott's insolent attitude aside, after Gillard's speech, I began a little research into "misogyny". I did a bit of reading and spoke to both men and women and folks of various levels of education and political orientations. And alas, in spite of my good intentions, I found I wasn't much clearer about it.

Instead, my mind turned to some familiar territory. I've always had an interest in history and in particular royalty, and by some quirk the Gillard speech got me thinking about how misogyny might manifest in the monarchies of the world, both past and present.

I turned my attention to a few famous monarchs and discovered that quite a few of them would these days be considered either misogynists or sexist, if not both. These explorations helped me, I believe, to come to a better understanding of what misogyny is, and more.

This book shares that journey with the reader. It is a kind of historical kaleidoscope not limited to misogyny but covering all sorts of misconduct and naughtiness in a number of selected noble circles, all viewed from the mischievous perspective of an ordinary bloke (that's the author).

The cases illustrated are mainly selected from the British royal family and a few from the French monarchy. The tales are portrayed in a satirical manner and the depiction of the particular cases is focused on the more "spicy" aspects of the happenings rather than on the historical importance of the events.

For those who like a bit of "seasoning" and controversy, be assured that sexual themes, adultery and the like are frequently present throughout the book. Political correctness is not.

In addition to the particular examples, there is a selection of supplementary material and also some trivia and even a few jokes which will hopefully make the reading lighter and more entertaining. A couple of sections about horoscopes and their credibility are also included.

Writing a book in which misogyny is a central feature without mentioning mothers-in-law (MILS) would be weird, so there are also a few fragments about these otherwise wonderful human beings who are so often unfairly embattled and complained about.

Though much of the additional data deals with anatomic sex, grammatical gender and "the battle of the sexes", not all of it is necessarily related to misogyny.

I should also clarify that the book is not intended to analyse misogynist behaviour or its roots from a psychological or psychiatric perspective. That would be a task rather suitable for someone resembling Sigmund Freud or the like, and which, even if I were qualified to accomplish it, I would find very boring and uninspiring. When saying this, I realise there are a countless number of folks in this world who would strongly disagree with my assertion.

I will end the introduction with an auto-criticism. Having completed the book, while checking the text again, only by glancing at its title, I immediately got disillusioned with myself. Why did I name it "Kings, Queens and the Sordid In-between"?

Even without bothering to give the book a fair go, its title may suggest to some that from the very outset, the story is biased towards misogyny. Otherwise, why isn't it titled "Queens, Kings, and the Sordid In-between"? Why didn't I put the fair sex first?

Ladies and gentlemen (at least here, I used the proper order!), if I did that, I suspect that certain groups in the broader community might find the "fair sex" term offensive and patronising. To me, the sequence of kings followed by queens sounds a more natural idiom, so I'll leave the title as is and hope that the gist of the book won't antagonise too many women, or men for that matter.

Terminology

At times, the terms England and Britain and English and British are loosely used throughout this book. Strictly speaking, when speaking of the monarchies of Britain the word British should only be used when referring to kings and queens that ruled after 1707, or to events that happened after that point in time.

In 1706 and 1707, under the reign of Queen Anita, two separate Acts of Union were passed by both the Parliament of England (which included Wales and Cornwall) and Parliament of Scotland, thus creating the unified sovereign state of Great Britain.

Before that, in 1603, on the death of Queen Libby I of England, her nephew, Jimmy VI of Scotland had united with Jamie I of England and Ireland, thus merging the crowns of England and Scotland. That had been just a unification of the monarchies of the two countries, or a dynastic union.

My apologies, please. I am told that Queen Anita should be referred to as Queen Anne; that Queen Libby I was rather known as Elisabeth I and both Jimmy and Jamie were actually the same dude known as King James VI of Scotland and James I of England.

Well, if my arithmetic serves me right, James VI plus James I still makes two Jameses or, perhaps James VII, but

I don't wish to quarrel and be stroppy, so I will accept the corrections.

After the 1603 dynastic unification, England and Scotland had continued to operate distinctly, with each having their individual judicial, religious and sexual education systems. Sorry – I am corrected again. It should read just *educational systems*.

More than a hundred years later, the 1603 dynastic union was formalised by the legal unification of 1707, when England and Scotland merged under the same Parliament, sitting in London with Yes Minister. Sorry – with Yes Minister should read *at Westminster*.

A further Act of Union in 1801 added the Kingdom of Ireland to establish the United Kingdom of Great Britain and Ireland. However, in 1922 Ireland effectively seceded from the United Kingdom to become the Irish Free State, while at the same time Northern Ireland broke away from the Irish Free State to re-join the United Kingdom and subsequently, the United Kingdom changed its name to "The United Kingdom of Great Britain and Northern Ireland", typically shortened to The United Kingdom, UK, or just Britain – names which we normally use these days.

To be exact and correct, the terminology used in this book should always consider the above events. But that's only if you are pedantic, or an historian, or a pedantic historian.

Otherwise, from my observations, I've noticed that ordinary folks like you and me, typically use in the day-to-day speech the terms English and British interchangeably.

In case any present or future members of the British royal family get hold of this book, I hope they won't be slighted by the occasional mix-up of terminology.

That's not saying they won't have other reasons to be affronted about.

But maybe they won't. This book is meant to be semi-comical and, as far as I know, the people of the Old Fart have a good sense of humour.

Oops! Did I just say "Old Fart"? Sorry, I meant to say the *Old Dart*. I only recently learned that the "Old Dart" is Aussie slang for the "Old Country", which is England. Well … it's England or perhaps it is Great Britain. Whatever …

Anyway, to avoid confusion, it is probably more sensible not to refer to the people of England or Britain as English or Brits. How about Poms? With any fuck, the use of the term "poms" should not offend anyone. Sorry – I meant to say any *luck*.

Misogyny and Misandry

Talking about kings and queens, there are too many instances in history where royal behaviour has been absolutely shocking and appalling, dreadful and deplorable. These days, some would add one more adjective to the list, or maybe two – misogynist and sexist.

In Australia, the term "misogyny" became fashionable during the period in office of Prime Minister Julia Gillard between 2010 and 2013.

On 9 October 2012 Ms Gillard delivered in Parliament the so-called "misogyny speech" in which she accused the Opposition Leader of sexism and misogyny. At the time it was widely reported in the media that Prime Minister Julia Gillard's fiery speech about sexism and misogyny has forced the word watchers to take note.

For those who may not be aware, when delivering the misogyny speech, Julia Gillard was the country's Prime Minister and Leader of the Labor Party. Relentlessly proud of the Labor's Party position regarding the equal treatment of women in the workforce, in politics and in society, nonetheless Ms. Gillard was forever delighted of her personal achievements in the eradication of sexist and misogynistic behaviour and attitudes, particularly in politics and also in the broader community.

Ironically, just a few years after the misogyny speech, in early 2016, a prominent Labor staffer named Stefanie Jones (photo below) unleashed a ruthless attack on her own party exposing a misogynistic culture within the ranks and accusing them of being "full of filth" and having a "disgusting attitude towards women".

Interestingly enough, Ms. Jones's anger was specifically directed at one of the Party's "heavyweights" namely the New South Wales Labor Party's General Secretary – Mr Jamie Clements.

Wow – what an impressive title! General Secretary! It reminds me of my thirty years spent in communist Romania, when the country's leader and Chief of the Communist Party also held the title of General Secretary and First Secretary of the Executive Bureau of the Central Committee of the Communist Party! The last man who held this title was the infamous Comrade Nicolae Ceausescu. He was also the President of Romania and Supreme Chief of the Armed Forces.

Back to Ms. Stefanie Jones, previous page, following her allegations of sexual harassment against Mr Jamie Clements, the apparent perpetrator resigned his position. Wasn't that a sweet, clemency gesture from Mr Clements?

Back to the misogyny speech, following Julia Gillard's tirade, the Macquarie Dictionary has announced it was broadening the definition of the word misogyny to include "entrenched prejudice against women".

Checking the meaning of the pertinent terms in my dictionary, I found that misogyny was described as "hatred of women" while sexism was defined as "the upholding or propagation of sexist attitudes". As sexism was referenced to "sexist attitudes", I checked the meaning of the word "sexist".

Curiously, in my dictionary (which wasn't the Macquarie Dictionary) sexist was explained as "an attitude that stereotypes a person according to gender or sexual preference, rather than judging on individual merits".

My dictionary may be a little old, but still, that doesn't excuse defining the adjective "sexist" as being an "attitude" – which is clearly a noun.

This is like defining the adjective "brainy", for example, by referencing it back to a noun. For instance, the definition of "brainy" could be expressed as follows: "The first woman Australian Prime Minister who held office between June 2010 and September 2013 and became famous for her October 2012 misogyny speech in Parliament".

While this hypothetical definition has the merit of capturing Ms Gillard's greatest achievement during her time in office – that being the misogyny speech – referencing the adjective brainy back to a proper noun, that being a certain Australian Prime Minister, still doesn't make any sense; — does it?

Anyway, perhaps when "sexist" was explained in the dictionary as "an attitude", the preposition "of" was inadvertently omitted from in front of "an attitude".

Now, those responsible for rewriting the dictionary, argue that "sexism" seems to be moving towards the surface features of the perspective and "misogyny" applies to the underlying attitude. Misogyny is similar to sexism, but "with a stronger edge to it".

One aspect not specifically spelt out in the definition of misogyny but usually implied in day-to-day usage and meaning, is that misogynist attitudes are mostly displayed by men.

It was certainly what Ms Gillard was getting at in her misogyny speech; the Opposition Leader being – at least on face value – a man.

But wasn't Ms Gillard's furious attack on the Opposition Leader a classic example of misandry? In case some of you wonder, misandry – a very rarely used word – means hatred of men. Both misogyny and misandry come from the Greek "misein", which means hatred. In Greek, "gyne" means women and "andro" is men.

So, was the now dismissed Prime Minister right to feel unfairly treated by her male politician colleagues for the only reason that she was a skirt? Sorry – I meant to say that *(sometimes)* she was wearing a skirt? Would it have made any difference if she wore a kilt? Given her partial Scottish background, maybe she once did wear one.

Anyway, regardless of whether she wore a skirt, a kilt, trousers, a miniskirt, or even nothing at all, perhaps the reason for Ms Gillard's downfall was that she had nothing to show. Neither in a hair salon, for example, nor in Parliament.

Trivia:

Two of the highest IQ's ever recorded in history belong to women. One of the women is American magazine columnist Marilyn vos Savant. No wonder Marilyn is so smart – she is a "Savant" after all! Savant? That's a Scholar, philosopher and/ or thinker. Nothing to do with politician!

Misogyny or Incompetence?

In Australia, like in most countries on Earth whether they be democracies or otherwise, traditionally the head of government was always a man.

This fait accompli lasted for some 110 years, from the time when the Federation of Australia was formed in 1901 until 2010 when this very motivated lady named Julia Gillard – deputy Prime Minister at the time – decided that enough was enough and put her hand up for the top position as the first ever female Prime Minister of the country, backstabbing in the process the male incumbent PM who'd been in the job for less than three years. His name is Kevin Rudd.

A groovy achievement and motive for huge celebrations – many of us would have thought; particularly if we were women. It so happened however, that the newly installed lady PM was anything but crowd-pleasing to her constituents regardless of their being blokes or broads.

Perhaps the scorn most folks expressed for Julia Gillard had something to do with her pathetic betrayal of the former Prime Minister whose job she took in 2010 and her lamentable performance in the highest office, but her advisors and Cabinet mates concocted other reasons.

In short, they said the sun shone out of her backside and her dung smelled of roses. The obvious and only reason she was disliked (by men) was that she was a "feisty" woman.

Parenthetically, she once described herself as a "strong feisty woman" by comparison to the Opposition Leader whom she labelled a "policy weak man". As man is the antonym of woman and weak is the opposite of strong; is the suggestion here that "policy" is the opposite of "feisty"? That's how it reads – and again, it doesn't make much sense, as feisty is an adjective and policy is a noun. It does sound like a brainy Prime Minister.

Though opinion polls showed that women in the electorate hated Ms Gillard's guts as much as men did, the "misogynist plot" in Australian politics was so conceived that, with the PM herself vehemently entertaining this conspiracy theory, the intrigue gained momentum and persisted right to the time when an election was held.

Even after Julia Gillard lost the 2013 election, many of her supporters blamed her heavy defeat at the polls on the tragic detail that she had been born a woman. Some said that men wouldn't vote with her because she's got more brains than all the males on Earth, bipeds included.

Being it fact or anecdote, men were apparently jealous of her wits. Women were also green with envy because of Julia's gorgeous looks and overall chic appearance, particularly her hairstyle. No wonder – her boyfriend was a coiffeur, after all. For those who have never seen the lady before, a photo is provided below. If you don't like the photo, there is another shoot of Julia towards the end of the book.

But, that is enough and even too much about Julia Gillard – at least for the time being.

Let's move from Aussie arse-kissers to British royalty.

Sorry, I meant to say *baby-kissers*. I'll start with one of the latest additions to the UK's royal family – one who one day, will very likely be the King of Britain and sovereign of our country too.

Before we move on, there is some trivia below. Please be assured, I would never suggest that either a cockroach or a nymph could in any way be associated with a former Australian Prime Minister.

Trivia:

Do you like cockroaches? Not a lot of people do and actually most of us hate them. Take this description of cockroaches for example: "Vile little crawling, flying, swimming bastards who have come from Satan". It says it all.

Or, figuratively, a cockroach is a "derogatory term used to describe individuals with poor honour, character or reputation".

Given that cockroaches are undoubtedly much hated creatures, should we have a word defining hatred of cockroaches? We do have the term misogyny describing hatred of women and, one should hope, women aren't loathed any more than cockroaches are.

So, if we agree that we should have a term labelling hatred of cockroaches, what should that word be? There is actually a word describing fear of cockroaches and that term is "katsaridaphobia". Nice one, isn't it? But "fear" is not the same as "hatred".

But why did I ask if you like cockroaches? You'll see in a tick.

How about nymphs? Sometimes mistaken with mermaids and sirens, nymphs can be described as a symbol of beauty and romanticism. In Greek mythology a nymph is a female deity or goddess eternally depicted as young and gorgeous. A nymph is also defined as a spirit of nature always envisaged as a beautiful maiden.

Did you know that a nymph is also a baby cockroach? I didn't, until recently. The question that bothers me is why on Earth a nymph, which is a creature known by definition as being a female, should ever be associated with a roach?

But, perhaps women shouldn't feel awfully bad about such an association. Let's not forget that a roach is a beetle after all. And hey, has anyone ever in this world been more famous than a Beatle?! John Lennon himself once said he was more popular than Jesus!

Now, how about another word derived from "nymph", which in effect means "woman with hot pants"? That is a nymphomaniac. As far as I know, there is no word to describe a man with hot pants. A man with hot pants is … just a man with hot pants. Isn't this discrimination? It obviously is. The only other question is who in this instance is the target of discrimination? Is it Men or Women?

Talking about goddesses, in Hindu religion "Kali" is the "goddess of motherly love". The same Kali is also the goddess of death, violence and sexuality. What a great combination! Back to goddesses, I don't mean that they are nymphomaniacs, though perhaps Venus or Aphrodite could be. Roman Venus and her Greek equivalent Aphrodite are the goddesses of love, beauty and pleasure after all!

A Timing Difference that May Prove Meaningful

On the morning of 23 July 2013, just when I turned the radio on to listen to the 5:30 am AEST (Australian Eastern Standard Time) news update, the presenter announced that Prince William's wife – Catherine Elisabeth, Duchess of Cambridge – had given birth to a baby boy. The boy – later named George Alexander Louis – is now third in line to the British throne.

It was reported on that Tuesday morning that the royal offspring, born in the Lindo Wing of the London's St Mary's Hospital – the same place where Princess Diana gave birth to Prince William and Prince Harry – was in good health and weighed 6 pounds 8 ounces, or 3.8 kilos. Not bad.

Some more details followed but what attracted my attention was the day and time the little fella was born. In London the birth took place at 4:24 pm (16:24) on Monday, 22 July. Due to the daylight saving time operating during summer, the real time the prince was born was actually 3:24 pm (15:24).

Taking into account the real time difference between London and Sydney (10 hours if the daylight saving time is disregarded), it means that, translated to Sydney time, the future king was born at 1:24 am next day – on 23 July.

Had George Alexander Louis been born at 1:59 pm (or 13:59) London time, which is just 85 minutes earlier, the Sydney time would have been 11:59 pm (or 23:59) on 22 July and the official date of his birth of 22 July would match in both London and Sydney.

But someone up there seems to have complicated the things – perhaps a little more than a little. Because it's not only the day of his birth that differs in London and Sydney – it's also his star sign. According to Western astrology, in London the prince is a Cancer, while in Sydney he would be a Leo.

Is this perhaps a hint from the skies, or a sign from the stars? It could well be. And if it is, the sign might indicate that right from his birth, Prince George is not on the same page with us Aussies. If so, how should this divergence be interpreted?

It might tell us that once the prince becomes one day the King of Britain it will be time for our nation to part ways with its mother country.

That's what the republican movement strives for, but this is not necessarily good news for them or, not in the short term anyway. As the prince's grandfather and father hadn't had a shot at the royal seat yet, it might take quite a few years for Prince George to be crowned king and for Australia to become a republic.

It seems the majority of us believe that following the birth of Prince George Alexander Louis, there will be a boost in the pro-royalist sentiment matched by a hitch in the republican movement. The April 2014 visit by Prince William with wife Kate and royal offspring George Down Under did not help the republican cause either. On the contrary – it may well cause a glitch in their campaign that could take some decades to recover from.

The fact that the little prince's star sign is Cancer but he'd have been a Leo if born at the same point in time but in a different location, like Sydney, or many other places on Earth for that matter, prompts me to digress a little into the topic of star signs and horoscopes.

(Above: Prince George Alexander Louis)

Before that, let's not forget that now the little Prince has a little sister. That's right – on the second day of May 2015 the legendary stork delivered Charlotte Elisabeth Diana, Princess of Cambridge, daughter of William and Catherine, now fourth in line to the British throne, after Prince Charles, Prince William and her older brother, Prince George.

Princess Charlotte was born at the very same St Mary's Hospital and, at 8 pounds 3 ounces, or 3.71 kilos, she was nearly as heavy as Prince George. That's not as heavy as

Prince George is now – it is the prince's weight at the time when he was born.

The time of Princess Charlotte's birth was 8:34 am London time. Because of the daylight saving time operating during summer, the real time the princess was born was actually one hour earlier, or 7:34 am. That's 5:34 pm (or 17:34), same day in Sydney.

So, in terms of both date (day) and star sign, Princess Charlotte's time of birth is consistent in London compared to Sydney. No trouble with Princess Charlotte, which makes sense – doesn't it? I mean if we, Down Under, become a republic during Prince's George reign and assuming Charlotte makes it to the throne as well, she'll surely rule after him, which won't affect us Aussies at all. By then, we should be a republic already!

(Above: Charlotte Elisabeth Diana, Princess of Cambridge)

Are Horoscopes Credible?

Many millions of us; probably hundreds of millions, believe that the star sign is a chief pointer which shapes or at least inspires one's character and prospects in life.

That's why so many dupes spend every year a heap of dough to hopefully uncover ... well – poor mugs believe if they spend a little fortune on clairvoyants, they'll hopefully learn about a vast fortune coming their way.

So, is this dough really wise spending?

When talking about horoscopes, one very dubious thing is the credibility of the tales given by so-called clairvoyants, whom I also dub psychos. Apologies – I am told psychics is the more accepted word. I'd thought psychic and psycho was the same.

How about warlock, sorcerer, wizard, or bitch? Sorry – I meant to say *witch*. Are these so-called professions also part of the same kinfolk? I guess they are.

So, horoscopes are built on astrology, which is allegedly a science. In brief, astrology studies sex positions and aspects of human bodies during love affairs and intercourse in bed.

My apologies – it looks that I got the definition wrong. I am told that astrology studies the *position* and *aspects* of heavenly bodies in the belief that they have an influence on the course of natural events and human affairs occurring on Earth.

Well, I wasn't too far off the mark. I mean some human bodies are heavenly. Take Megan Fox, for example. And love affairs are human affairs and beds are on Earth after all. And, if astrology is a science, many would argue that sex is an art.

Anyway, they say there are many versions of horoscopes based on different calendars and zodiacs and other stuff. The ones most commonly used are the Chinese Horoscope and the Western Horoscope.

To reinforce the above point, I will emphasise that both the Chinese and Western horoscopes are not based on the sex position of the partners at the time one was conceived, but on the position of the planets and stars at the time a bloke or a sheila was born. Is that clear enough?

As the position of the stars used to predict one's future and fortunes in life is taken at one particular time – that being the time of one's birth – you would think that a horoscope is, or should be, set, permanent and predetermined for each human being and for the duration of their life.

Keeping the above aspect in mind, I have a heap of trouble accepting or trusting the yearly, monthly, weekly, or daily horoscopes published in a variety of mags and on the Internet.

Perhaps the architects of these "updated" predictions would argue that the fundamental horoscope, given by the position of one's star sign is permanent and remains valid for the life of the subject, while the other periodical forecasts differ from the primary one in the sense that they are given at a more in-depth level of nitty-gritty.

As a person's lifespan is made up of a number of years, which in turn comprise a number of months and weeks and days and so on, the argument may sound clever. I am however skeptical that the aggregate of these sub-horoscopes reconciles back to the fundamental one – and this quiz can only be tested when the subject of the horoscope kicks the bucket.

Actually, there are a myriad of cases when a particular event which happens in one's being – most times not predicted in that individual's star sign – will change their life forever. More often than not, such events are tough luck.

While I don't read horoscopes on a regular basis, I can definitely say that I never saw in any publication one such prediction of bad luck; and still misfortunes happen every day of the year; indeed every minute of the day.

From what I have seen, bad luck is usually only very subtly hinted at and the words are carefully chosen so that the potential targeted group doesn't get nervous when reading about what their fortune within a particular timeframe might be.

It is human nature that we don't like to learn bad things about ourselves – though many of us get a kick when reading or hearing of misfortunes as they relate to others. Negative news sells the papers, they say, but this doesn't apply to horoscopes.

Talking about the most common versions of horoscopes, it is noted that all twelve star signs under the Chinese horoscope are named after beasts.

I am sorry to say that, having just glanced at the names of the star signs, the underlying misogynist and discriminatory mentality embodied in the list stunned me. It is obvious that some 5,000 years ago, the Chinese didn't give a hoot about political correctness either. I mean the feminine gender they just utterly ignored.

For example, the Chinese have Ox as a star sign, but there is no Cow. Further, they have Tiger, but no Tigress and there is Rooster, but no Hen. I guess some would claim that having no hen is not such a bad thing after all. With no hen, one wouldn't bother screwing their brains trying to answer the ever bamboozling dilemma of what came first – the chicken or the egg?

On top of the other bigotries, the Chinese have a Dog Star sign, but where's the Bitch?

Sure, some of the names given to Chinese star signs are commonly used for both male and female animals and such are the Rabbit, the Horse, the Goat or the Monkey. Still, I'm afraid that's not good enough. As an absolute minimum, they should have the Bitch as a star sign in its own right.

The Western star signs are marginally more compliant with political correctness guidelines, but that's only compared to the Chinese ones. The Aries star sign for example also means Ram. Why not Ewe? The Taurus is also a Bull. But what's wrong with the Cow?

Anyway, there are millions and probably tens of millions of dupes who believe in these regular predictions and I must admit, when my missus buys or receives a mag in the mail that includes a star signs segment that is the first section she examines.

Having said that, I am not trying to convince others that horoscopes are nothing more than glorified crap. Should I attempt to do so, I would be at loggerheads with my dear wife and she is the last person on Earth I would dare to take on.

Even so, I am not the only one who finds that the same horoscope applying to a large group of folks belonging to a particular star sign lacks credibility. I mean there are more than seven billion of us on Earth, or some 600 million people in each star sign, and these are huge numbers.

Suggesting that in matters of family, love, money, work, health and so on, the very same things will happen to all 600 million of us in any given period, like next year, next month or next week, for the only reason that we were born within a 30-day or so timeframe, I find as credible as flying pigs.

I suspect that even the authors of such forecasts know very well that their predictions lack credibility. This might be a reason why they keep the prophecies so general and many times so vague and uninformative.

I took the time to check some weekly prophecies in a particular magazine which I won't name and here are some examples of the findings below. Some predictions are not only very vague, but perhaps ... let's say, mysterious, or just too shrewd to understand. And to me, most, if not all of them, reveal ... well – absolutely nothing.

Selected horoscopic predictions below are in italics and there are also short remarks underneath each of the prophecies.

Selected Weekly Horoscopic Forecasts

From 8 to 14 May, 2010

Gemini

You'll get fulfilment through working behind the scenes and helping others.

Comment: Hmm ... What does this mean? Is it like working behind the scenes to get jobs for the boys, for example? Or being fulfilled while working behind the boys?

Leo

Lack of progress regarding career will be replaced with momentum and promising developments.

Comment: You mean career as in clairvoyant? Indeed, I'm looking forward to promising developments, but that's your career.

Scorpio

You'll be surprised at how easy life is when you're willing to compromise.

Comment: Could you define what easy life is in this context? I suppose being a clairvoyant is easy life.

Aquarius

You have an acute understanding of people. As a result, you'll be able to provide others with comfort and advice.

Comment: I certainly don't have an acute understanding of what this prediction implies. Not even a dull grasp of it. To put it politely, I have no effing clue of what you are raving about.

From 14 to 20 May, 2011

Gemini

An important message or opportunity will be delivered in a very subtle way.

Comment: What is subtle way? Is it like the way this prophecy is formulated? Too subtle for me, thank you.

Leo

This is a good week for a career boost – you just need to show some initiative.

Please do that! Your career certainly needs a boost.

Sagittarius

Positive stars in your health sector will make you feel physically and mentally fit.

Comment: I sure experienced both physical and mental fitness that particular week from 14 to 20 May. My diary shows I spent most of it in bed with the flu and felt absolutely miserable.

From 7 to 13 April, 2012

Libra

If you haven't made plans to take the road less travelled, what's stopping you?

Comment: I don't own a freaking car! And nor can I afford to rent one. Not even a bicycle!

Sagittarius

Are you feeling the love? You should find yourself overwhelmed with support and positivity.

Comment: I am not feeling the love. No one gives a shit about me. Not even mum fancies my mug.

Aquarius

Self-expression is more important than ever. Let your individuality shine!

Comment: Yeah – I just told my boss what I thought of her. The cow gave me the boot.

Pisces

If you haven't made the most of Mars in your relationship sector, it's time you take the bull by the horns and challenge people's perception of you.

Comment: Isn't Mars the Roman God of War? I did just that – tried to act like Mars – I mean, in a belligerent manner. It got me nowhere. Actually it got me in an interminable queue at Centrelink applying for the dole. See above.

From 20 to 26 July, 2013

Libra

It's time to mingle, dance, romance and do all the things Librans excel at!

Comment: I might be a Libra, but, more importantly, I am a Libra-Ryan! My middle name is Ryan. And Ryan doesn't mingle or dance in the library! Otherwise, he doesn't excel at anything.

Aquarius

The full moon in your sign heralds a milestone or an exciting new era.

Comment: Yeah – that was the week when Centrelink rejected my application for the dole. It was very exciting.

Gemini

The full moon highlights your belief system prompting you

to leave past hurt behind and look ahead.

Comment: What's this supposed to mean? If you're hinting at religious beliefs, having been left penniless, I don't believe in celestial generosity anymore.

From 7 to 13 September, 2013

Libra

If there's something to clear up or get off your chest, act now.

Comment: Yeah – I am doing that right now – swearing a lot and with passion while reading your crap!

Sagittarius

You may want to set the record straight, particularly with colleagues or bosses.

Comment: Done it and got a kick in the arse. See above.

Taurus

Live a little! Kick back, reward yourself and don't take life too seriously.

Comment: I'm not that keen to make the same mistake twice. I am a tad nervous that if I kick back, I might get another kick in the back.

Cancer

Follow through on bright ideas, especially those that involve making money.

Comment: This suggestion is absolutely genital! Sorry, I meant to say *genial*, as relating to the genius adjective. Why hasn't anyone ever thought of that before?!

From 9 to 15 November, 2013

Capricorn

Socialising will help you blow off steam, as well as meet valuable contacts.

Comment: Yeah, I did that the other night. I went to a farty party. That is a party where you just sit around and fart. I certainly blew plenty of steam.

Pisces

With vivacious Venus in your social sector, you'll be in the mood to party!

Comment: You mean that Venus? The Roman goddess of love? I know her meanings em-body beauty, love and sex – all that in a gorgeous body. I wouldn't have thought Venus was the goddess of partying. Or, are you suggesting an orgy?

Virgo

Been a little tongue-tied? Now you'll be able to express yourself effectively.

Comment: You mean tongue-tied as in inarticulate, incoherent, unintelligible, incomprehensible, stuttering, and so on? I am all of these. So, with such serious tongue deficiencies, how am I going to suddenly express myself effectively?

From 14 to 20 December, 2013

Gemini

The full moon in your sign heightens your sensitivity and need for attention.

Comment: Hmm … that's a good one! Here, the comment that comes to mind is the politician Pauline Hanson's much satirised answer when she was asked by a reporter if she was xenophobic, back in 1996. Her response – "Please explain" – became a much parodied catchphrase in Australian culture. So, dear clairvoyant – please explain!

From 15 to 21 March, 2014

Taurus

You'll feel idealistic and think of ways to make the world a better place.

Comment: Yeah, I did think of a way. I am joining a Utopian Socialism association if one still exists.

Gemini

Use the Full Moon in your home sector to give your surroundings a complete overhaul.

Please explain!

Cancer

You'll finally get something that has been eluding you.

Comment: I wish I could find a horoscope that made at least a scrap of sense. But it's still eluding me!

Aquarius

There is no escape from making a decision, so don't try!

Comment: That's right – I just made the decision to never-ever read effing horoscopes again!

From 29 March to 4 April, 2014

Taurus

It's time to let go of the past and recharge your batteries.

Comment: What do you mean? Perhaps go on a honeymoon? Where would I get the freaking money?

Remember – I've got no home, no car, no dough and I'm still out of work! I don't even have a wife, or a prospective one. As a devoted queer, I am the wife!

Cancer

Make the most of your enthusiasm and ambition to forge ahead.

Comment: Even if I were enthusiastic, could I possibly forge behind?

From 12 to 18 April, 2014

Gemini

Let go of outdated goals and make room for new aims.

Comment: You mean new aims or Aimées? I only know one Aimée and she's gorgeous. I guess several Aimées would be fantastic!

Virgo

This is a good time to look at pooling your resources with someone.

Comment: What resources are you talking about? I've already told you I've got no home, no car, no dough and no other assets. The only capital I have is me and that's not much of an asset either.

Pisces

Sure you have the funds and the desire, but think twice before spending.

Comment: That's not quite true. I certainly have the desire to spend, but got no freaking dough! How many times do I have to tell you?!

Misogyny Flares into a War that Lasted a Hundred Years

If anyone believes that the demise of Julia Gillard was a tragic consequence of misogyny, how about all the trouble the hatred of women has caused between England and France in the Middle Ages?

Even the Hundred Years' War – which actually lasted 116 years between 1337 and 1453 – can be blamed on misogynist attitudes in medieval France; attitudes which were so entrenched in the kings' mentality that they had been incorporated in Frankish law in as early as the 6th century.

With the Salic Law forbidding women to rule the country as queens, when the throne of France became vacant in 1328 and no obvious male successor was on hand the English used the chance to claim the crown for themselves.

The trouble began some 700 years ago when in 1314, French King Philip IV the Fair called it quits. None of his three sons who followed him in quick succession was able to procreate. Or, rather none of his daughters-in-law ever delivered a male.

Perhaps conceiving kids was not a serious proposition for at least two of the women daughters-in-law to the king, as, early in the 14th century, Margaret of Burgundy and Blanche of Burgundy were keeping themselves occupied entertaining a couple of Norman knights in their boudoir. The boudoir was actually the Tour of Nestle, where the orgies allegedly took place.

Possibly, the prospective queens were taking the pill to make sure they wouldn't get impregnated while playing around with non-royals. Whatever the reason was their inability to conceive a boy caused another tragic case of misogyny taken to extreme.

By 1328, when Philip's youngest son Carol IV died, there was no male descendant to the royal seat. I will repeat myself stressing that the Salic succession law prohibited females and their descendants from inheriting the crown! How dare the Frogs do that?!

Quite possibly it happened because at the time they didn't have a Parliament in the current meaning of the word. Had they had a modern political institution like we have today, it would have certainly included some Green senators of which a few would be very vociferous females.

They would have made sure that any Salic, relic or whatever succession law operating at the time, was abolished as to permit talented women to mount the throne.

Note: Recalling that Poms refer to the French as "Frogs", I used this alternative word above. Subsequently, I learned that Frog, as a substitute for French, is actually offensive. I didn't bother to change it, as it sounds quite suitable to me.

Instead, I took the liberty to go even further and used below the idiot "Croaker" when talking of the French. Sorry – I didn't mean to say *idiot Croaker*. I meant *idiom Croaker*. Croaker is a synonym for Frog, after all. And these French Frogs do croak a lot, don't they?

So, the French succession saga didn't have a happy ending. That's because, in addition to his three sons, Philip the Fair also had a daughter – Isabella – married to King Edward II of England. Hard and determined, this Isabella was born ahead of her time.

In passing, when I said Isabella was hard, I meant hard as in firm.

To continue the very boring saga, while the French mob of barons installed Charles IV's cousin – Philip VI of Valois – on the throne, Isabella with firm boobs had different ideas. She claimed the Croakers' crown for her son, Edward III.

The French screw of nobles told Isabella to get stuffed; they quarrelled and continued with insults and that's how the Hundred Years' War began in 1337. The rest is … history, as they say.

Sorry, I mistakenly said above the French screw of nobles. I meant to say *crew of nobles*.

I won't venture into telling how a war that lasted 116 years went. You probably know the yarn anyway and would get bored to tears if I did.

I will however comment that the war went on, and on, and on … under the headship of five English kings and an equal number of five French kings. These were consecutive monarchs, not concurrent. To the credit of sheilas, there were no female queens either in England or France during that turbulent time. A few of the male kings may actually have been queens, if one was to lean into some fabulous connotations.

But seriously, except for Joan of Arc, the ladies did not

participate in the brawl. And Joan wasn't a lady anyway. I mean she wasn't a woman of polished family background or upbringing.

Actually, Joan of Arc wasn't Polish either. She was just a Frog country lass and later she became a saint. No disrespect for Joan; it's just an observation. I should hope no one could ever disrespect a saint. But why isn't Joan of Arc referred to as a saintess?

Trivia:

The Hundred Years' War ended in 1453. At that time, in England, Henry VI was ruling, while in France, Charles VII was the bully. Interestingly, both Henry VI of England and Charles VII of France reigned within the same very exact period between 1422 and 1461.

More intriguing, the next kings who followed in England and France – Edward IV and Louis XI respectively – both ruled within the same precise timeframe, from 1461 to 1483.

Back to Isabella, indeed, she was a stiff sheila and didn't accept naughtiness. Isabella was actually the one who divulged her sisters-in-law's love affairs with the Norman knights. Then, having attained severe puniwshment for Margaret and Blanche's indiscretions, Isabella, while married to the English King Edward II, took herself a lover! That's leading by example, as they say.

The fucky chap was Baron Roger Mortimer, Earl of March. Sorry, I mistakably said fucky. What I meant to say was that Mortimer thought he was *fluky*.

He wasn't. Poor dupe – also married at the time when he hooked up with Bella – wasn't so blessed after all. Perhaps, being the dad of a dozen kids, he began to date Isabella because he was superstitious to the point that, had he continued to hang around his missus, he'd probably father a 13th offspring with her, which was ... bad lick and not only in England. Sorry, I meant to say *bad luck*. And it was bad luck anyway, as it turned out.

Perhaps, when Isabella took a lover, she should be pardoned because of mitigating circumstances, some would argue. It was common knowledge at the time that her hubby, King Edward II, better enjoyed the company of the male sort.

So belle Bella was sitting at home lonely and apparently unutilised. Which makes you wonder – was Edward III, the claimant to the Croakers' throne – indeed the offspring of King Edward II?

One could also rightly wonder why Edward II, while knowing that he didn't fancy dames, still married a woman, and even worse – he married a French woman. I mean, according to anecdotal evidence, compared to their English counterparts, French women are said to be very naughty. That's what the gag below suggests as well.

A Frenchman was accused of having had sex with a dead woman. In the Court, though he admitted his guilt to the Judge, he exonerated himself saying, 'I swear your honour; I did not know she was dead. I honestly believed she was English.'

Anyway, Isabella's love affair with sweetheart Mortimer didn't go too well. The two of them did however force Edward II to abdicate and, in 1327, allegedly, arranged his murder – an act to which Edward II's heir – that was Edward III – took affront. The boy, who wasn't fifteen yet when made king at the time of Edward II's passing, swore revenge. He kept his word.

In 1330, he had Mortimer hanged for ... whatever reason. Apparently it is said to be for treason. And the young king didn't stop at that. He put his mummy under castle arrest though it wasn't a severe punishment, or imprisonment.

Isabella was billeted in the Castle and it is alleged that, being blue-blooded, the ex-queen was fed with Blue Castello brie. She wasn't even billed for being billet-ed in the castle. No, that's not true – I just made it up. But what is true is that royals always have it so easy!

Isabella died in 1358 aged 62 or 63, while the Hundred Years' War, which she had instigated, went on for another 95 years. The events leading to the Hundred Years' War, including Isabella's shrewd machinations behind the scenes, briefly mentioned above are brilliantly presented by Maurice Druon in "The Accursed Kings" series of historical novels.

Trivia:

In 1327 Edward II was the first English king forced to abdicate. In total, there were five English monarchs in history who relinquished the throne, either being coerced to do so, or of their own accord. These were:

- Edward II in 1327
- Richard II in 1399
- Lady Jane Grey in 1553
- James II in 1688
- Edward VIII in 1936

Mary Stuart, Queen of Scots was also forced to abdicate in 1567. There is a separate section about Mary Stuart later in the book.

Regnal Numbers

Back to Prince George Alexander Louis, once he'll ascend to the throne, he will be given a self-styled regnal number. Regnal numbers are ordinary numbers which distinguish monarchs (or Popes for that matter) from others of the same (first) name and who held the same title in the same jurisdiction.

Sorry for mistakenly saying above that regnal numbers are ordinary. I meant to say they are *ordinal numbers*. Nothing about royals could be ordinary. Extraordinary – yes!

So, when Prince George Alexander Louis's turn to the throne comes, he will be styled King George VII. Presumably, before that, his grandfather, Prince Charles will reign as King Charles III followed by Prince William, who would be King William V.

Speaking of Charles, is there anyone who still believes that the poor chap will ever be king? As it stands now, it seems "an impossibility in its purest form".

And leaving Charles aside (as his mum did long ago), it is important to note that these regnal numbers are unique only within the same jurisdiction, being it kingdom, empire or papacy.

Confusion can arise when naming a certain monarch without specifying his realm or territory. For example, there has been a King Henry IV of England (1399 – 1413), a King Henry IV of France (1589 – 1610) and also a Henry IV, King of Germany and Holy Roman Emperor (1056 – 1106).

There have also been two English Kings named Charles, seven French Kings named Charles and seven Holy Roman Emperors named Charles as well. There were also a few kings Charles in Spain and ... probably, somewhere else.

Though it seems unlikely that Prince Charles of Wales will ever be King Charles III of Britain, he could console himself dreaming that once, he was ... maybe King Charles III of France.

But, maybe Charles' missus wouldn't fancy that wish as King Charles III of France was known as "The Simple" and Camilla wouldn't like her Charles to be any simpler than he already is.

Perhaps Carolingian Emperor Charles III would be a better proposition. No way! Camilla would protest, because that Charles III Emperor was branded "Charles the Fat" and these fat fops have a bad reputation. That is, in the erotic department.

Is there a king homonym (meaning the same name) for Prince William – like King William V? I couldn't find a homonym for King William V, but there have been quite a few *homo kings*, one could say if we were to play with the alliteration.

Anyway, you've got the idea that these regnal numbers can be obscuring. And, if this type of confusion is not sufficient, in both England and France for example, historians have added more muddle to the system of regnal numbers.

In France, the starting point of the Frog monarchy was the year 987 with King High Carpet of the Carpathian dynasty. Sorry – that should read *Hugh Capet of the Capetian dynasty.*

By contrast to the English numbering system of monarchs where certain kings with the same name were not given a number or sequence, in French history, kings that reigned before 987 were numbered, thus causing a different type of confusion to the ordinary bloke on the street. And I assume, to sheilas as well, not only to blokes.

When reading a record of French monarchs, you'll find that the first Louis king listed is actually Louis VI the Fat (1108 – 1137) and the first Charles is Charles IV (1322 – 1328). Similarly, the first Robert is Robert II the Pious (996 – 1031), but the first Henry is rightly Henry I (1031 – 1060) and the first Philip is indeed Philip I (1060 – 1108). Perplexing is saying the least.

Confusing numbering of kings though is not the most perturbing matter when talking about English and French monarchs. There have been times in history when kings of England aspired and claimed parts of or even the whole realm of France. See the Hundred Years' War, above, for example.

Eight Edward Kings instead of Eleven

By the early 7th century, England was divided into seven Anglo-Sucks-on kingdoms. These were East Anglia, Yes-Sex, Kunt, Merci Beaucoup, North Umbria, Suss-Sex and West-Sex – with each of the seven kings fighting for supremacy over the whole cunt. Sorry, I meant to say the *whole country*.

It wasn't however until early in the 9th century when Stefan Edberg, who had become King of West-Sex in 802, was accepted as ruler of all England (827).

Sorry, the first King of England wasn't Stefan Edberg; his name was *Egbert*. Nonetheless Stefan Edberg was crowned King of England, when he won the Wimbledon tennis tournament, and twice for that matter, in 1988 and 1990.

Thus, year 1988 is considered by many historians as the point in time when the history of English monarchy began. That's wrong – it was actually year 827. Others believe Alfred the Great (871 – 899) was the first king of a unified country.

Either way, there is consensus that the history of English monarchy began sometime in the 9th century. For the purpose of this book, year 827 is taken as the point in time when the English monarchy was founded.

My apologies! It seems that mixing up the years and the magnificent country of England with … something …

still magnificent but, hopefully not as ... vast as the whole country, wasn't my only error in this section of the book. Checking the above list of the seven kingdoms that formed ancient England, I just realised that I made a mess of it.

First, those seven realms were Anglo-Saxon, not Anglo-Sucks-on. And of the seven Sex-Sates of England, I only got one right. That was East Anglia, but I made another blunder in the meantime. Sex-States should read Estates or alternatively, Ex-states.

The other 6 six kingdoms, or territories, or domains, or Ex-States, or Estates or ... whatever should read as follows:

No matter how desperate one is to have sex in the area north-east of London, Yes-Sex is not the correct title of that region. Its proper name is Essex.

And, no matter how much one is craving to have a ... I'd better rephrase this ...

Let's start again. The area in south-east England right near the Channel Tunnel is actually named Kent, not Kunt. That's rather obvious; isn't it? I mean, we always say Duchess of Kent, not *Duchess of Kunt*. Got it?

And Merci Beaucoup should read Mercia. Well, merci beaucoup for fixing that, but that's only four names I corrected, so I still got three wrong.

No big drama with North Umbria. It should actually read Northumbria, but that's pretty close. Northumbria is in Northern England and North Umbria ... well, it should indicate the Northern part of Umbria, which is in Central Italy, some 2,000 kilometres away. That's pretty close.

Then, you have probably sussed out that Suss-Sex doesn't stand for "dubious sex", but was supposed to read Sussex. What would dubious sex be, anyway? Possibly doggy sex? Sorry again – as suss is a synonym for dubious, and dubious can be a substitute for dodgy, I meant to say *dodgy sex.*

And lastly, West-Sex doesn't stand for wild sex (as in the Wild West). It should read Wessex.

Now, that we've clarified this regrettable mix-up, I'll add that from the 9th century to the present day, there have been quite a number of English kings and queens named Alfred, Anne, Charles, Edgar, Edmund, Edward, Elisabeth, George, Harold, Henry, James, John, Mary, Richard, Stephen, Victoria and William. The list includes only the so-called common names.

In addition to these, there have been kings with less usual names, like the already mentioned Edberg (or Egbert); then Athelstan, Canute, Edred, Edwy, Ethelbald, Ethelbert, Ethelred, Ethelwulf and Hardicanute.

Short time or disputed monarchs like Matilda and Lady Jane Grey should also be mentioned. As both of these were women, we could otherwise be accused of misogyny.

From the time when Alfred the Great died in 899 to the Norman conquest of 1066, there have been three English kings named Edward. These were Edward the Elder (reigned 899 – 924), Edward the Martyr (975 – 978) and Edward the Confessor (1042 – 1066).

However, none of these Edwards was ever given a regnal number, order, or sequence. I mean, shouldn't Edward the

Elder be known as Edward I? Shouldn't Edward the Martyr remain in history as Edward II? And shouldn't Edward the Confessor be referred to as Edward III?

It should, one would think, but it wasn't like that. In addition to these three "forgotten Edwards" above, there are eight Edward kings numbered in the history of England after the Norman conquest of 1066 and the first one, or Edward I, only started his reign in 1272. This is nearly 400 years after Edward the Elder, which should have been the rightful Edward I in 899.

Shouldn't this wrongly numbered Edward I actually be Edward IV and Edward II be Edward V and Edward III be Edward VI and so on? This way, there would be eleven Edwards instead of eight and the last one would be Edward XI instead of Edward VIII. That's how it should be, but that didn't happen.

Why didn't it happen? It appears that in English history, kings only began to be numbered after the Norman conquest of 1066. But why is this? If it is generally accepted that the history of the English monarchy began sometime in the 9th century, why were kings only numbered starting two centuries later?

Well, does it really matter if there are eight instead of eleven Edward kings? one would ask. It probably does matter.

As it stands now, both Edward and Henry are the most common names of kings listed in British history. There are eight kings named Henry and an equal number of eight Edward kings.

If Edward kings had been numbered starting with Edward the Elder, then Edward would be the most popular name of all English kings. With names other than Henry – those being Charles, William and George – currently the next ones in line to the throne in this order, it is likely that Edward would still remain the most popular name of all British monarchs for a long time to come. This is unless Prince Harry would have his turn at the throne as well.

Should Prince Harry ever succeed to the throne, things would get a little complicated. Being the first ever Harry, would he be referred to as King Harry I, or just King Harry?

We know that King Stephen of Blois (reigned 1135 – 1154), wasn't given a regnal number, as he was the only English monarch ever named Stephen. And so was King John Lackland (1199 – 1216) and even the more famous Queen Victoria (1837 – 1901). She was just Victoria, not Victoria I.

With Harry however, there is a further complication. That's because at first, the name Harry started out as a nickname for Henry and even today Harry and Henry are generally considered the same name, though Harry is increasingly becoming a name in its own right. The popularity in recent years of JK Rowling's hero Harry Potter has probably played a part.

Even though Prince Harry himself is very popular, particularly with young ladies! Prince Harry, however, was christened Henry Charles Albert David and formally styled Prince Henry of Wales. So there seems to be no doubt that if becoming king, Prince Harry would, after a break of some 500 years, reinstate the series of Henry kings as King Henry IX.

Let's hope he wouldn't be as conspicuous as the last of the Henry kings – the notorious Henry VIII (1509 – 1547).

Thus, given that three Edward kings have never been assigned a number, in the event that one day Prince Harry becomes king, Henry would overtake Edward as the most popular name of all English monarchs. This couldn't possibly happen if all Edward kings had been assigned a regnal number starting with Edward the Elder at the turn of the 9th century (see above). However, the probability of Prince Harry becoming king seems pretty slim for the time being. Since Princess Charlotte Elisabeth Diana was born on 2 May 2015, Prince Harry has now been dumped to fifth in line to the British throne, presently.

Talking about Henry and Edward kings, isn't it curious that the very last of the Henrys and also the last of the Edwards (these being Henry VIII and Edward VIII) have been the most controversial of them all?

Henry VIII
(1491 – 1547; reigned 1509 – 1547)

We mostly remember Henry VIII for marrying six wives, of which he slayed two (had this anything to do with misogyny?!), for his insatiable appetite for both tucker and dames and for, possibly most notably, his breakaway from the Catholic Church which led to the introduction of the Protestant religion in England. I personally think of him as one of the stinkiest monarchs in European history.

Henry's decision to retreat from Catholicism was prompted by the Pope's refusal to give him a divorce from his first wife, Catherine of Aragon – daughter of the Spanish Catholic Monarchs Ferdinand of Aragon and Isabella of Castile.

Henry desperately wanted a son and Cate only produced stillborn children, a few kids who died prematurely and a daughter – the future Mary I of England.

To add a bit of clamour to the story, before Henry VIII, Cate had been married to Henry's older brother, Arthur, Prince of Wales – heir apparent to the English throne.

Cate and Arty married in late 1501, but sadly, less than five months later, the young prince died, aged just fifteen. Perhaps it was because of a broken heart. Many historians believe that at the time of Arty's death, Cate was still a virgin; others think the opposite.

Apparently, Arty and Cate couldn't understand each other as they spoke different versions of Latin. Whether this tongue barrier acted as an impediment in their intimate relations … I wouldn't dare to speculate. Perhaps Cate, feeling guilty of possible accusations of paedophilia, was waiting for Arty to become an adult. We'll probably never know.

Even today, the question of whether Cate's marriage to Henry's brother was consummated or not still remains a subject of controversy. It seems unlikely though that, regardless of what side of the story they supported, any historian at the time actually examined Cate's … thing to deliver a warranted judgement.

Henry himself wasn't sure either if, when he first slept with Cate, she was an experienced partner or not. Pending his personal agenda, he first maintained that Cate's marriage to Arty had not been consummated. Later on, when he wanted a divorce from her, Henry claimed the opposite, arguing that having slept with Arty and then marrying him (Henry), Cate had caused her marriage to Henry to be invalid on the grounds of incest.

So, in 1509 Henry and Cate married but it was pretty clear

that, following the 1516 birth of their daughter Mary, by 1525 Henry had lost all his patience and was sick of his first missus because the cow wouldn't conceive a boy.

Nevertheless, it is obvious that, in addition to being sick of his wife, the king was also sick in the head. In other words, the fuckwit king was certainly "mental".

Trivia:

It is said that late in his life Henry VIII suffered from diabetes, endocrine problems, syphilis, hypothyroidism, leg ulcers, muscle weakness, and, according to some accounts, paranoia, anxiety, depression and mental deterioration. By the time of his passing he weighed close to 400 pounds, or about 180 kilos!

A possible excuse for Henry was that in Spanish, "esposas" means both "wives" and "handcuffs". And Catherine of Aragon was certainly Spanish.

It is also worth noting that in 1509, when Cate married Henry VIII, she was nearly 24 while Henry – six years her junior – hadn't turned eighteen yet. So, Cate perhaps hadn't learned a lesson from her own past paedophilic mistakes. This was going to haunt her in later years.

Anyway, the age difference wasn't Henry's motive to ask for a divorce. By 1526 he was already besotted with Anne Boleyn and deeply troubled that the foxy gal wouldn't sleep with him because … she was probably playing hard to catch.

By contrast to Anne, her sis, Mary Boleyn, hadn't had any such qualms when she became Henry's mistress. She was married too, while having it off with the king!

Obviously frustrated, Henry resolved he had to divorce Cate, but Pope Clement VII refused to annul the marriage. Apparently the Pope was cautious not to affront Europe's most powerful monarch at the time – Habsburg Emperor Charles V, who was Cate's nephew.

Trivia:

Speaking of Charles V, below are some interesting coincidences that marked important events in the life of the greatest ever Holy Roman Emperor.

Charles V was born on 24 February 1500 in the Flemish town of Ghent.

On 24 February 1525 – the very day he turned 25 – Charles scored a humiliating victory over his archrival's (French King Francis I) army in the Italian town of Pavia. I am stressing the victory was humiliating because the French soldiers outnumbered the Habsburg army by about five to one and the French king himself was taken prisoner.

On 24 February 1530 – the day Charles turned 30 – Pope Clement VII crowned him Holy Roman Emperor in the Italian city of Bologna. The Pope must have been very slack. Charles had already been Emperor for more than ten years!

It is noted that Charles V was the last Emperor to be crowned by a Pope until, nearly 300 years later, Napoleon Bonaparte bashed Pope Pius VII, bullying the Pontiff into making him Emperor.

Charles was the eldest son of Catherine's sister Joanne of Castile, better known as Joanne the Mad. In 1554 Charles's son – Philip II of Spain, who was a first nephew of Mary

I of England – married none other but his aunt, Mary I of England!

Weddings between close relatives part of royal families across Europe were not a strange proposition during those times. It was rather weird if royals did not marry a close relative.

Sadly, like her mother had done before, Mary I also failed to produce a boy. In fact, to the disgust of her hubby Philip II of Spain, she didn't conceive any kids. She only faked pregnancies and died lonely in 1558, aged 42.

We'll talk some more of Mary I and also of Henry VIII's other offspring later in this book. Let's first take a brief look at Henry's six wives.

Catherine of Aragon
(1485 – 1536; queen consort 1509 – 1533)

As already pointed out, Catherine's parents were the revered Catholic monarchs Ferdinand of Aragon and Isabella of Castile. What hasn't been revealed yet is that Ferdinand and Isabella were blood related but, being a marriage between royals, this detail is probably implied.

Ferdinand and Isabella were actually second cousins. How else could a royal marriage in those times be properly constituted unless the parties were closely related?

The Pope's dispensation to deal with consanguinity was never a serious barrier at the time. In this case, it was Pope Sixtus IV who duly gave his endorsement to the royal union. It is also noted that, at the time of the wedding, being aged eighteen, Isabella was an adult, but Ferdinand, one year her junior, was still underage.

Back to Catherine of Aragon, born in 1485: she was the youngest surviving child of Ferdinand and Isabella. Incidentally, 1485 was the year when the Tudor dynasty, to which Cate was later to become an innate part of, ascended to the English throne.

In what was a remarkable achievement, in 1507 Cate was appointed ambassador for the Spanish Court in England, becoming the first woman in European history to hold the ambassador title.

Perhaps it was ambassadress at the time, but because of new political correctness guidelines, women's titles must be displayed as being equal to men's and, accordingly, a former ambassadress is now a female ambassador. (See "Feminine and Masculine Common Nouns" chapter later in this book).

So, what's an ambassadress? Well … it's obvious, isn't it? It's an ambassador wearing a dress.

Henry though wasn't impressed with the former ambassadress. That's because he was sexually obsessed. Sorry – he was that as well, but I meant to say he was obsessed with *conceiving* a son to carry on the Tudor male lineage of monarchs.

Henry's paranoia caused a huge amount of bother in England – a fuss which remained in history known as "the king's great matter". Given that Henry's second missus grumbled about his "manhood" and that he remained non-physical with at least two other wives, maybe the king's great matter wasn't so great after all.

On the topic of achievements, it is noted again as an even higher accomplishment, that 503 years after Catherine of Aragon was named ambassador, Ms Julia Gillard became the first ever woman Prime Minister of Australia.

Another attainment of … I was about to say of Julia Gillard, before realising in time that Ms Gillard's becoming the first woman Prime Minister of Australia was actually her only achievement. Sorry, I apologise! I was forgetting the misogyny speech!

Let's start again. So, another incredible success of Catherine of Aragon was her 24-year marriage to Henry VIII. Wasn't that length of time she survived in the company of the mentally disturbed king utterly remarkable?

Cate's matrimony to Henry was actually by 10 years longer than Henry's total duration of his other five marriages added together. By contrast, Cate's marriage to Prince Arty of Wales – Henry's older brother – had lasted only 20 weeks.

A further triumph, which Cate didn't live to see, was that the girl to whom she'd given birth in 1516 was later to become the Queen of England – that was the forthcoming Mary I of England, also known as Mary Tudor or Bloody Mary.

Catherine died in 1536, aged 50. Had she lived to see her daughter on the throne of England … perhaps she wouldn't have considered that a great triumph.

In short, it is said that Cate was highly intelligent, caring, gracious and charismatic. A painting in the early 16th century portrays her as a young woman of the finest beauty.

Catherine was always faithful and ardently loved her husband – King Henry VIII – despite his womanising and else despicable ways. Did the disgusting buffoon deserve such a wonderful wife? He probably thought not, when he ditched Cate and took five more wives afterwards.

Anne Boleyn
(1501 or 1507 – 1536;
queen consort 1533 – 1536)

It was touched on above in the "Henry VIII" section of the book that when the king fell in love with Anne Boleyn, she rejected his advances and refused to go to bed with him.

But seriously, did Henry VIII ever fall in love with a woman? That's probably just sheer imagination. As far as Henry VIII was concerned, to him, falling in love invariably meant "I wanna screw you babe!" It is true however that, though he seemed incapable of truly falling in love with a woman, every day Henry was becoming more and more enamoured of himself.

So Anne wasn't head-over-heels with the king and told him off, but when Henry craved for something, he could be and was very persuasive.

Apparently, it was Anne's "pert young duckies" that Henry treasured the most and itched to play with and kiss. It seems that "duckies" is a medieval term for a woman's breasts.

Like a besotted teenager would do, Henry wrote Anne a number of passionate love letters solemnly promising to make her "his sole mistress, rejecting all others".

How many other mistresses were to be discarded? We'll probably never know for certain. Anyway, that promise of Henry must have been quite flattering to Anne!

Finally, by late 1532, Anne gave in to Henry's erotic desires and in early 1533 she was pregnant with the king's offspring. In spite of the Pope's refusal to give him a divorce from Catherine, in January 1533 Henry secretly married his new sweetie.

His act baffled quite a few as Henry had now become a bigamist! And more, Anne wasn't a glam broad either. Some say she had six fingers on one hand and moles all over her body. Others maintain she had six fingers on both hands and even three breasts. That could explain why Henry cherished her boobs the most.

In May 1533, persuaded by Henry, the Archbishop of Canterbury pretended to hold Papal powers and declared the king's marriage to Catherine of Aragon null and void. A few days later, Anne was crowned queen, which prompted the real Pope to excommunicate the king. No one at the royal court gave a hoot about the Pope's action.

In September 1533 Anne gave birth to the future Queen Elisabeth I. It is not known how old Anne was at the time.

Some historians claim she was born in 1501; others believe Anne's year of birth was 1507.

It's not even known which of the sisters – Mary or Anne – was the older. Nor are historians sure which of the women was younger! The only certain thing is that, at different times, both women enjoyed the king's intimate favours.

Perhaps enjoyed is not the right word in this context – it isn't a secret that Anne herself once complained of Henry's poor performance in bed and of his weak "manhood".

It is noted that, before sleeping with Anne, the king had found her foxy, but once he lost his lust for her, to him, Anne was suddenly boring and fugly.

The gender of newly born Elisabeth bothered the king quite a lot, so at the time of her birth, he took offence at the Queen for being as insolent as to produce a broad and again, began to indulge himself with bedding other ladies. How he did that with his weak manhood remains a mystery.

Still, Anne fell pregnant again. Whether by Henry or not, is not exactly known. What is acknowledged is that aged 41, the king was already whinging of consistent bouts of impotence. And Viagra was not available at the time.

In 1536 Anne prematurely gave birth to a son. Sadly, the boy was dead, which infuriated Henry. Incidentally, the miscarriage happened on the very day when Henry's first wife, Catherine of Aragon was being buried. Was that a divine intervention or just the spell of a scorned woman?

Henry's verdict of Anne's failure to carry on with her pregnancy was that his second marriage was cursed by incest too. This time he blamed his love affair with Anne's sis – Mary Boleyn – as the grounds for the incest. At the time of Anne's miscarriage, Henry was already courting his next wife-to-be, Jane Seymour.

Ironically, though Catherine was already dead, her former loyal courtiers turned against Anne calling her "the concubine" and "whore". No doubt feeling isolated and in an attempt to gain support, Anne began to flirt, which prompted rumours that she had taken lovers. Impatient to marry Jane Seymour, Henry himself entertained the gossip.

To cut the long story short, Anne was arrested, charged with high treason, incest and adultery and found guilty. When she was executed in May 1536; she was either 28 or 35. Less than a fortnight after Anne's execution, Henry VIII married his new belle, Jane Seymour.

Jane Seymour
(c 1508 – 1537;
queen consort 1536 – 1537)

Unlike Henry's previous wives, Jane – born in about 1508 – was not as highly educated. She could read and write only a little, but was very good at household work. Jane's needlecraft was testified to be outstanding. Physically, she is said to have been of average height and quite plain-looking and to have had a modest personality.

Talking about modesty, when referring to his political rival Clement Attlee, Winston Churchill once said that he, Attlee, had all the reasons to be modest about.

Back to Jane Seymour: though she had been in Henry's depraved court for several years, it was alleged at the time of the marriage that she was still a virgin. Perhaps that was just a fable. Knowing Henry VIII's reputation, it is hard to believe that, having met the king, any of the young ladies at the royal court could possibly have remained a virgin afterwards.

In spite of rumours that at the time of marrying Jane the king was already impotent, nine months after the wedding, it was announced that she was pregnant. Perhaps the king's alchemists had, in the meantime, discovered a sort of predecessor to Viagra?

The most fascinating event about Jane's pregnancy was that she developed a craving for quails, which the king certainly understood.

He'd had, over the years, cravings for a countless number of quails. (Incidentally, "quail" is also slang for a woman or girl.) For Jane however, the king duly imported real quails (i.e. birds) from both Flanders and France.

On 12 October 1537 Jane gave birth to a baby boy. That was Henry's long-awaited son – the future King Edward VI. But Jane, after birth, fell gravely ill. She died less than two weeks later.

The exact cause of her death is not known, but it had certainly something to do with the birth of Edward VI. The boy, from an early age, was always unfit and sickly.

What was unique about Jane was that she was Henry's only missus who didn't share her name with any of his other spouses. Two of his other wives were Anne and three were named Catherine.

Trivia:

Jane Seymour will probably be best remembered by the Poms for playing Bond girl Solitaire in the James Bond film Live and Let Die. That was in … 1973. It must have been a much more pleasurable experience than playing queen consort to Henry VIII. No wonder – Solitaire's bed partner was heartthrob Pom actor Roger Moore.

If you think that playing a Bond girl is not an honourable role for a queen … well, maybe it's not, but at least Jane didn't play in the "Octopussy" movie and nor did she play Bond girl Pussy Galore.

Jane Seymour (photo below) also played French Queen Marie Antoinette, mentioned later in this book. Well, perhaps I should add that the woman who featured in the above roles was *actress* Jane Seymour.

And, if anyone is puzzled about the two Janes, it looks like it was Jane the actress who deliberately caused the confusion. Her real name is actually Joyce Frankenburg. Why did she decide to change her name? It's possibly because she thought Frankenburg was uncomfortably similar with Frankfurter and, if that was the perception, "Hungry Henry" might well have eaten her.

Leaving the entertainment aside and back to serious matters, incredibly, after Jane's death, Henry remained single for three years. During that time, he mostly devoted himself to eating and, as he wasn't bulky enough, he put on stacks of weight.

Nevertheless, by the age of 48 and most probably by then totally impotent, Henry was ready to marry again and have one more shot at fathering another boy – brother to ailing Edward. His fourth wife, whom he married in early 1540, was German-born Anne of Cleves.

Anne of Cleves
(1515 – 1557; Henry VIII's wife for six months in 1540)

Anne, born in Germany in 1515, is said to have lacked education and artistic refinement; instead, she was kind-hearted, honourable and subservient – qualities handy to possess by any potential partner of the demented king.

Contemporaries described Anne as tall and slender, blonde and having a lovely face.

Henry though, thought she was a sort of troglodyte, or perhaps he just used that epithet as an excuse to justify his failure to ever penetrate her.

The cow didn't even speak English and, on top of lacking sexual education, the "Cleves" broad was also poor in the "erogenous cleavage" department, which may have aroused the king, if she hadn't been deficient. Her boobs were droopy and slack! That was according to Henry.

Less than six months after they married, the king, already repulsed by his new wife, ordered Anne to leave the royal court. Soon after, the matrimony was annulled on the grounds that it was never consummated. Well, I assume that was the discreet way of putting it. They couldn't have stated in the divorce papers that the freaking king was a hopeless impotent sort!

Oddly enough, after the divorce, Henry and his ex became best friends, with Anne being referred to as "The King's Beloved Sister". It appears that such a reference was devised as a tardive explanation of why Henry had remained floppy when sharing his bed with Anne. I mean royal incest was typical for kings in those times, but not so often with their own sister.

In addition to not being penetrated by the king, Anne of Cleves is remembered in history as Henry's only wife who was not crowned queen consort. When she died in 1557, Anne had outlasted Henry and all his other wives.

Having terminated his marriage with German born Anne on 9 July 1540, the king very quickly moved on. On 28 July the same year, Henry VIII was married to Pommy-born Catherine Howard.

Catherine Howard
(c 1523 – 1542;
queen consort 1540 – 1541)

It seems Catherine, born in about 1523, was too emancipated for those eras. She is said to have taken her first sexual partner at 13 or 14 and, from a very young age, she was apparently a proficient lover and even enjoyed "communal sex".

So, what's scandalous or weird about communal sex? Excuse my ignorance, but as I understand it, "communal" means shared, joint or mutual. I mean isn't sex supposed to be shared, joint or mutual? Well, I am told there are some folks who better enjoy having sex solo. Now I understand.

Back to Henry, now at nearly 50, he took an interest in his fifth wife-to-be when she spotted the young, attractive Catherine in her role as lady-in-waiting at Anne of Cleves' court.

It is interesting that, aged about seventeen, when the already experienced Cate went to bed with Henry the king never complained that she wasn't a virgin. Perhaps it was just in his imagination that he copulated with the glam lass.

Though of Catholic faith, Cate was a first cousin of Anne Boleyn, who had been an Anglican. This detail posed a serious hurdle to Henry's desire of marrying the eye-catching Kate. The king's union with his second wife's first cousin was technically incest.

But who cared about that? When the king wanted something, the king got it. So the Archbishop of Canterbury arranged the necessary faked documentation and the marriage went ahead as planned.

But it wasn't to last. Young Cate was vivacious and vibrant and had an affinity for young and slim lads. King Henry was nothing like slim. At 50, his waist had ballooned to a huge 54 inches, or more than one and a third metres!

In early 1541 Catherine – who had brought plenty of "va-va-voom" to the royal court – was accused of having a lover.

And if that was indeed the case, was she to blame? I mean at her age, the poor woman needed regular servicing and Fatty couldn't deliver. What was she supposed to do? Go to an "Adult Shop" and buy herself a vibrator?

In late 1541 she was stripped of her titles, charged with adultery and imprisoned. Sadly, in February 1542 Catherine's life ended the same way as that of her first cousin's, Anne Boleyn – on the chopping block, aged just 18.

The execution didn't bother the king. Immediately after

the execution, he attended a copious supper with some 60 ladies present! He wrongly thought he still had in him a tiny bit of manhood left, but it wasn't quite enough for one more bed partner. His sixth and last wife was Catherine Parr, but she wasn't really a wife in the complete sense of the word.

Catherine Parr
(1512 – 1548;
queen consort 1543 – 1547)

Catherine, born in 1512, was a descendant of King Edward III. She was Henry's junior by 21 years. It is said that from an early age she excelled at studying and continued learning throughout her life. She spoke Latin, English, French, Italian and rubbish. Sorry – I meant to say *Spanish*.

Before marrying Henry in 1543, Catherine had been wedded twice and widowed as many times, so her virginity was not a question. Mind you, she could still have been a virgin, had her two previous hubbies been of the same calibre as Henry himself.

Certainly, Catherine and Henry had a number of common ancestors, making them multiple cousins on both their maternal and paternal lines. Perhaps this time Henry VIII used consanguinity as an excuse for his merely platonic relationship with his new queen.

With Henry quite old, sick and very fat, their marriage was rather boring. He'd given up the idea of having more kids and, even if he hadn't given up, he couldn't have done much about it.

He died in 1547, aged 55, while Catherine Parr remained in history as the most married English queen (four times). Even after Henry's death she married once more. This time it was her old flame Thomas Seymour – none other than brother of Henry's third wife, Jane Seymour!

Isn't it amazing how these royals always meddle in each other's lives? It is noted that, driven by ambition to advance his career, at various times this Tommy Seymour proposed to both Henry's daughters – the future Mary I and Elisabeth I of England.

Once Tommy also proposed to Henry's fourth wife – Anne of Cleves! That's after she was dumped by the king and began hitting the bottle. It would have come very nicely together if Tommy had married all three of them. As it turned out, he didn't wed any of the three. As it so often happened in those days, Thomas Seymour also ended up on the scaffold.

This time, it wasn't Henry VIII who ordered the execution. It wouldn't have made much of a difference. During his reign, Henry VIII had killed some 57,000 of his subjects, including two wives. His reign was plainly summarised by the rhyme below (author unknown):

King Henry the Eighth,

To six wives he was wedded.

One died, one survived,

Two divorced, two beheaded.

Trivia:

Have there been other infamous blokes in history even worse than Henry VIII?

There are a few candidates worth mentioning. A serious contender would be the brutal emperor of the Mongol Empire, Genghis Khan (born in about 1162; reigned from 1206 to 1227).

It is estimated that during their murderous campaigns, the Khan's troops killed more than 40 million people. That was more than any other mass killer in history, including Adolf Hitler.

Idiotically, these days environmentalists label Genghis Khan "the greenest invader in history", arguing that the decomposed corpses of so many people acted as a fertilizer causing substantial areas of cultivated land to grow abundant with trees and forests once again.

I find the above green comment not only incredibly inane, but of a very bad taste too. Give me a break, please!

On the issue of his associations with the other gender, it is said that the Great Green Khan owned a harem of more than 500 wives. So, compared to Green Khan, Fat Henry was just a little kid!

And, if you thought that Henry VIII was very bad, how about the great Zeus – King of the Gods in Greek mythology?

Zeus was such a legendary womaniser that attempting to list all his wives and mistresses would be a monumental task. It is sufficient to note that Hera – his most "permanent wife" – was also his sister. As conservative as that!

And Metis – another wife of Zeus – was also his cousin. Strangely enough, one day, feeling perhaps threatened by an old prophecy or maybe just hungry, Zeus ate Metis! This is true – it's not a typo or a spelling mistake. Zeus actually ate Metis. Perhaps he confused Met-is with Meat-is.

There was also King Solomon of Israel who reigned from about 970 to 928 BC. One of King David's sons, Solomon is renowned for his legendary wisdom. According to the Bible, Solomon had 700 wives and 300 concubines. Wise indeed he was!

Henry VIII's Siblings

The spiteful king had two brothers and four sisters.

The eldest of the seven siblings, Arthur, Prince of Wales (pictured below), was already mentioned in this book as first husband of Catherine of Aragon. Arty was born in 1486 and died in 1502, aged 15.

Margaret Tudor (next page), born in 1489, was the second eldest. In 1503 Maggie, who wasn't fourteen yet, married the King of Scotland, James IV. The Scottish king was more than fifteen years her senior. Another freaking paedophile! Their third son was the future King of Scots, James V, who was also Mary Stuart's daddy. Maggie died in 1541, aged 51.

Born in 1509, Henry VIII was only the third oldest, but certainly the weirdest of them all and by a long shot. He died in 1547, aged 55. Next was Elisabeth Tudor. Born in 1492, she died an infant, aged just 3 years old.

Mary Tudor (not to be confused with Mary I of England, or Bloody Mary, who was her niece) was the fifth of the Tudor siblings. Born in 1496, in 1514 Mary became the third and last wife of King Louis XII of France, who was nearly 34 years her senior! At least, Mary was an adult already, but only just – a few months into her 18th year.

Young Mary (above), renowned at the time as one of the most beautiful princesses of Europe, wasn't quite over the moon about her arranged marriage of state with Louis. She was in love with another chap and, at 52 King Louis XII was to her no more than an out-of-date, foolish match.

Luckily for her, but not for Louis, the king passed away right on the first day of 1515, less than three months into their marriage. It is alleged that, trying to please the lass, who longed to be pleased by a superman rather than a king, Louis had exerted himself too hard in the bedroom. It was one of history's lessons to old, silly fools still wearing hot pants. Sadly, Louis was to learn the lesson the harsh, tragic way.

Following Louis' passing, Mary didn't waste any time. In just a couple of months, she secretly married her beau. With a name suggesting a blend between Charles Bronson, Sir Richard Branson and perhaps Marlon Brando, indeed, Mary's darling must have been a sort of superman. His name was Charles Brandon, styled 1st Duke of Suck Folk. Sorry – it's actually *Suffolk*.

Mary and Charles had four kids together. Through her eldest daughter Frances, Mary was the maternal grandmother of Lady Jane Grey (see more about Lady Jane Grey later in this book).

Mary Tudor, younger sister of Henry VIII, died in 1533 aged 37. The sixth of the siblings, Edmund Tudor, Duke of Somerset, was born in 1499 and died the year after, aged 15 months.

Last of the siblings, Katherine Tudor, was born in 1503 and also died an infant, aged just about one week old.

Trivia:

There are innumerable unhappy husbands in this world who get sick of their wives and it probably happens on an even larger scale the other way around. But these days, divorcing is a very pricey business and so it was even centuries ago.

Well known for their entrepreneurial abilities, as early as in the 17th century, the Poms found a cheap, practical answer that got them around a very costly divorce. Not only was it cheap, it actually made them quite a bit of dough.

What did they do? Well, displeased British husbands simply sold their wives! The protocol was that the wife, led by a length of rope around her neck, arm, or waist, was paraded in front of a crowd of blokes and publicly auctioned to the highest bidder. As easy as that!

It was a successful trade at the time and would probably had been even more booming if a try before you buy clause had been attached to the sale contract. The practice went on until 1857.

If some think that selling one's wife was a misogynist act, others believe it was rather an amiable separation solution and innovative business venture.

Edward VIII
(1894 – 1972; reigned 1936)

In contrast to Henry VIII, who reigned for nearly 38 years between 1509 and 1547, Edward VIII held the English crown only for less than twelve months from January to December, 1936. His reign actually lasted for a mere 326 days.

It is weird to note that referring to Edward, his daddy, King George V, once said,

"After I am dead, the boy will ruin himself in twelve months". How on Earth did George V know that?

In spite of his very short time on the throne, Edward VIII arguably caused at least the same amount of controversy as Henry VIII had done some 400 years before.

Certainly, the Abdication Crisis of 1936 – when Edward

relinquished the throne to marry his sweetheart – was one of the greatest scandals ever to hit the British royalty.

Edward's downfall began when he was still Prince of Wales and in 1930 met a slender and stylish American sheila who utterly mesmerised the future king. Her name was Wallis Simpson.

At the time Wallis was still married to her second husband, Earnest Old-rich Simpson. Sorry, I am told his name was actually *Ernest Aldrich Simpson*. It appears this Aldrich may not have been so rich, or not rich enough to fulfil Wallis's royal ambitions.

Well, as it turned out, Edward wasn't able to fulfil Wallis either. Still, he fell hard (but not deep) for Wallis and, before being crowned king, he travelled all around Europe with his new mistress. Interestingly, the entire continent – and even America – knew about his love affair with Wallis, but the gossip was kept shush in England.

It wasn't until 3 December 1936 when the news of the king's affair with Wallis became public in London and the mob took it badly. Wallis who in the meantime had divorced, was insulted and ill-treated by the crowd. The king took the mob's reaction harshly too and pleaded with Stanley Baldwin – the country's Prime Minister at the time – to permit him to marry his sex kitten.

As passionately Henry VIII had begged the Pope 400 years before to let him get rid of his first wife, Edward VIII was equally fervent when imploring England's Prime Minister to allow him to get a first wife. But pig-headed Baldwin would have none of it.

Curiously, Winston Churchill was on Edward's side. At the peak of the crisis, Churchill was reported to have said: "Why shouldn't the king marry his cutie?" To which Sir Noel Coward – famous actor, composer, director, scriptwriter, singer and everything else – allegedly replied:

"Because England does not want a Queen Cutie". And the PM was in agreement with Coward. What a coward, indeed!

So, the king had to stay put. Though Wallis had come back to her senses and was prepared to abandon any claims on him, on 11 December 1936 Edward VIII made the extraordinary decision to exchange the British crown for a wedding ring which he put on Wallis's ring member.

Or, should I say ring finger? Well, as member is also defined as a limb, or appendage or extremity, ring finger and ring member should be the same thing.

But that's not that important. What's more thought-provoking is that she also put a wedding ring around his member, but it was too large. I mean the member wasn't too large, but the wedding ring was.

No, that's not what I meant to say either. He put his finger in her ... ring and she was pleased with it because the finger was larger than the member. Or, something like that.

But seriously, isn't the whole story ironic? I mean, by divorcing Catherine of Aragon against the will of the Pope, Henry VIII had proclaimed himself the Head of the Church of England – title which passed in time to all future kings and queens.

When rejecting Edward's plea to let him marry Wallis, the PM's refusal was based on the fact that Edward was the titular Head of the Church of England, which opposed the remarriage of folks if their former spouses were still alive, which in this case, they were – and two of them. I mean Wallis Simpson's first and second husbands.

It is actually not precisely known if Stanley Baldwin's opposition to Edward's marriage with Wallis Simpson was so fierce because Wallis was an American or because she was a divorcee. In either case, she was certainly a woman! Was Baldwin's refusal to consent to Edward marrying a woman another ludicrous misogynist act?

Well, during those times, the king couldn't have married a man, though it is said that, being poorly endowed to please women, Edward had also experimented with men.

Would it be possible today for a king to marry a man? The constitutional legality of this option hasn't been tested yet, as for more than 60 years, the Poms have had a woman on the throne. Some would however argue that the current Prince of Wales is married to a man.

Back to Edward, in addition to his forbidden affair and

subsequent marriage to Wallis Simpson, he also produced lots of hullabaloo because of his friendly attitude towards Adolf Hitler before and during World War II. Some historians have suggested that, had he won the war, Hitler would have reinstated Edward VIII as the king of Britain.

It didn't happen. What actually happened was that following his abdication, Edward was demoted from the supreme title of king to that of Dick. He was made Dick of Windsor. Sorry, that should be *Duke of Windsor.*

Wallis was also relegated from a "Simpson" – which some 60 years later, thanks to the animated television sitcom "The Simpsons", became one of the most famous families in the world – to that of … just "Warfield" – a name that doesn't have any famous connotations.

When changing her name in 1937 from Simpson to Warfield, Wallis didn't think it through. One single different letter in her newly chosen surname would have gone a long way.

Had she chosen to replace the "W" (as in Women) to a "G" (as in Gents), then "Warfield" would have become "Garfield" and her celebrity status would have lived on into the late 20th century and beyond through the comic strip "Garfield".

But, changing women into gents is probably not such a great proposition. Anyway, I hope my women readers won't think the suggestion had a misogynist motivation.

Following a 1937 tour of Nazi Germany, the Duke and Duchess of Windsor settled in France. Later Edward was appointed Governor of the Bahamas, a post that he didn't enjoy.

What else was there to do in the Bahamas – he would often complain – except for wearing pyjamas and eating bananas? Wallis didn't like their stay in the Bahamas either, but she did enjoy bananas.

A joke with bananas just came to mind:
At the greengrocer, two blondes bought three bananas. Frowning, the salesman put the fruit in a plastic bag and wondered aloud, 'Two women buying three bananas … It doesn't make much sense to me.'
'We'll eat one banana,' one of the blondes explained.

As for the Bananas as in the inhabitants of Bahamas, Wallis referred to them as lazy folks of a particular colour. How pathetic was that?! No awareness of equal employment, anti-discrimination, affirmative action, or political correctness – nothing of the kind!

Sorry – I am told that the locals in Bahamas aren't called Bananas, but *Bahamians*.

Both Edward and Wallis died in France. He passed away in 1972 aged 77 while Wallis lived on until 1986. She was nearly 90 when she died.

The moral of the story may well be that, if Edward VIII had not surrendered to the charms of Wallis Simpson, his younger brother George would never have ascended to the throne as George VI, which means that Elisabeth II would not have made it either. Now her name would only be a brief, ancillary mention in the history of British monarchy.

But we would have never known – maybe one way or another George would have made it to the throne, some could argue. Not if the underlying facts of life and death remained the same, others would counter argue. I mean, George VI died in 1952, while Edward VIII lived until 1972.

Indeed, if not for the obsessive infatuation of a king with a woman described by some as a "femme fatale with legendary talents", the history of England could well be very different today.

But having had Queen Elisabeth II for more than any other British king or queen on the throne, it's almost impossible to contemplate the British monarchy without her. She's now part of the scenery, like a piece of furniture seemingly sitting there since time began.

A Few Royal Statistics

While Queen Elisabeth II is currently the longest serving British monarch, her son – Charles Prince of Wales – certainly takes the cordon bleu! Since February 1952 the prince has been first in line to the British crown and, in April 2011, became the longest serving heir apparent to the throne.

No wonder that Charles is dubbed by some as The Forgotten Prince. But in the Queen's defence, at her age it wouldn't be unusual if she suffered from loss of memory.

Anyway, the Queen may have forgotten that she's got an exasperated son, but Prince Charles is certainly fully aware that his mother is alive, well and still reigning.

According to a comic television sketch which exposed his daily routine, the prince would wake up early in the morning, attend to the bathroom, eat breakfast, drink a coffee, read the newspaper and, not learning that the Queen had passed away, he'd then sit in an armchair for the rest of the day waiting for mummy Lizzie to die.

The stubborn nonagenarian however was always determined to break Queen Victoria's record as the longest reigning monarch in British history and she did so on 9 September 2015.

Below, in descending order, is a list of the seven longest reigning monarchs in the English and British history:

1. Queen Elisabeth II*
2. Queen Victoria – 63 years and 216 days
3. George III – 59 years and 96 days
4. James VI of Scotland and later James I of England – 57 years and 246 days
5. Henry III – 56 years and 29 days
6. Edward III – 50 years and 147 days
7. Elisabeth I – 44 years and 127 days

*As Queen Elisabeth II still held the crown as at 10 September 2015, she irreversibly surpassed Queen Victoria's record as the longest ever reigning monarch in Britain. At that date, she was 89 years and 142 days old. The much-trumpeted event was, most probably, not a motive for celebration for poor Prince Charles. He must have felt rather miserable on the day!

In European history Queen Elisabeth II is now the third longest reigning monarch behind Louis XIV of France, who fell asleep and forgot to wake up after 72 years on the throne (1643 – 1715), followed by Emperor of Austria, Franz Joseph I, who lasted for 68 years between 1848 and 1916.

Should Elisabeth II be as ambitious as to attempt to beat Louis XIV's record, she would need to live and sit on the royal seat until 2024. If Her Majesty reaches that milestone, she would be aged 98. She may not even remember her name by then, let alone that she was queen.

Comparing the reigns of Victoria and Elisabeth II, it is

pertinent to note that Elisabeth also has the upper hand over Victoria in terms of British Prime Ministers that served during her rule.

There have been twelve Prime Ministers in office since Elisabeth became queen. Of these, only one (Harold Wilson) served more than one non-consecutive term. There were also quite a few PM's that served consecutive terms, or more than four years during the Queen's reign.

It is of interest to note that, when Elisabeth was made queen, the incumbent British PM was none other than the famous Winston Churchill. He had already been in that job during the tumultuous period 1940 to 1945.

Born in 1874, Winston Churchill lived for 26 years in the 19th century. Born in 1926, Elisabeth "missed" 26 years of the 20th century.

One of Elisabeth's PM's was a woman – and what a woman she was! Sure, that was the "Iron Lady", aka Margaret Thatcher.

By comparison, there have been ten prime ministers who served during the reign of Queen Victoria. Of these, six served more than once. None of Queen Victoria's prime ministers was a woman.

So, in terms of misogynist attitudes, antidiscrimination, affirmative action, political correctness and so on, Elisabeth wins again.

In respect to certain physical attributes, Queen Elisabeth II also prevails when compared to Queen Victoria. It has been documented that Queen Victoria measured four foot eleven inches in height, or 149.86 centimetres. Queen Elisabeth II is allegedly 5 foot four inches tall or 162.56 centimetres. So our contemporary queen is by 12.7 centimetres taller than Victoria. In the imperial system that's exactly five inches.

The above evidence proves once more that it is much comfortable to be blue-blooded born and get a job for life as monarch than to pursue a politician's career.

I mean, can you imagine an 'ordinary chap or a sheila being prime minister for 60 years?! Or, can you picture the country's head of government being about 90 years old and falling invariably asleep during the Question Time institution of Parliament?

(Mind you, it doesn't mean that our incumbent PM is not dead to the world during any Parliamentary sessions.)

As a last hypothetical question, how about having a nine-year-old kid as the prime minister of the country? I am sure many would argue that an underage boy or girl would do a better job than Australia's current prime minister and certainly much better than the last – and only – female PM. By the way, at the time of writing this book, Australia's prime minister was Mr Malcolm Turnbull.

More, you don't need any remarkable qualities to hold the royal crown and, apart from the occasional quarrels and brawls about a potential disputed succession to the throne, as king or queen you'll have no opposition.

Even the average man on the street could make an outstanding monarch and so probably could a woman on the street.

But not quite so if you aspire to be prime minister. Not only need you to win your seat in parliament and also come on top in an election; you must also exhibit some essential personal qualities both before the election and after – while exercising your duties.

First of all, as prime minister you must be a complete, accomplished liar!

English and British Queens

In nearly 1,200 years since King Egbert in 827, there have been four English queens and three British queens ruling over England and the United Kingdom (see list below). So, four plus three makes seven queens. On average, there was one queen for each 170 years.

Compare this to the total number of kings and you'll find that the boys have outnumbered the girls by nine to one. I won't hint of misogyny again. The facts speak for themselves.

It is also noted that, for a short period of eleven years between 1649 and 1660, England was a republic, so there were no kings or queens during that time.

The English queens, who ruled before the 1707 union between England and Scotland, were as follows:

- Lady Jane Grey, known as The Nine Days Queen – reigned between 10 July and 19 July, 1553
- Mary I – reigned between 1553 and 1558
- Elisabeth I – reigned between 1558 and 1603
- Mary II – reigned from 1689 to 1694

The British queens, who ruled after the 1707 union were:

- Queen Anne – reigned from 1702 to 1714*
- Queen Victoria – reigned from 1837 to 1901

- Queen Elisabeth II – the reigning monarch since 1952

*Queen Anne reigned both before and after the merger between England and Scotland. It was during her rule that the union took place.

Isn't it odd that the first three of the English queens listed above ruled consecutively over a short period of 50 years from 1553 to 1603, while the four remaining queens are scattered over a timeframe of 327 years from 1689 to present (and still counting)?

For those who believe misogyny is and has always been a genuine problem, it may be of interest to note that since the history of English monarchy began in 827, it took more than 700 years until a woman was first crowned queen in 1553. All 42 previous monarchs before then had been men. No comment!

Although in 1141 Matilda – daughter of Henry I – was for a very brief time elected Lady of the English, she was never crowned queen. Nevertheless, Matilda is often referred to as Empress Matilda. This title should not suggest that she was ever Empress of England or of Great Britain. It is a title she attained when she married Holy Roman Emperor Henry V.

Next chapter is a little yak about the Pommy queens and also about other famous or less famous monarchs in English and British history.

Matilda
(1102 – 1167) – short-time Lady of the English

Though not technically a queen, Matilda, the only daughter of King Henry I (youngest son of William the Conqueror), deserves a remark. Matilda's mother was also a Matilda and there was also a third Matilda (of Boulogne – see below).

Matilda was just eight years of age when she was betrothed to German King and later Holy Roman Emperor Henry V, whom she married in 1114 at the age of twelve. Henry was only sixteen years older. (Was that a lawful wedlock or rather another disgusting case of paedophilia?!)

When Henry V died in 1125, Matilda, still only 22 years old, was left childless and lonely. By then she'd grown into a "hot redhead" adored by her German subjects. But she preferred French.

In 1128, she married French Geoffrey Plantagenet, Heir to the Count of Anjou. One more blunt example of paedophilia? It seems so, as at the time, Geoffrey – Matilda's junior by eleven years – hadn't turned fifteen yet!

The death of Henry I's only son in 1120 had made Matilda the sole legitimate heir to the throne of England. It wasn't that Henry I didn't have any other offspring; he had plenty. Throughout his life, his flock of mistresses had yielded him some 25 children, but all were illegitimate.

In 1127 Henry had compelled the powerful gang of barons to accept Matilda as his successor, though a woman ruler was unprecedented for the kingdom of the Poms.

In 1135 Henry I died because he'd stuffed himself with too much fish. The barons, in spite of their promise to support Matilda, declared Stephen of Blois (grandson of William the Conqueror and a cousin of Matilda) as King of England.

Just like that! Only because this Stephen had balls and the misogynist barons (and liars as well!) could not stand having a sheila in charge! Even the Pope himself – Innocent II – supported this Stephen lad. Sorry to say it, but I can't see how Pope Innocent was innocent!

Matilda did not despair. Helped by her half-brother Robert of Gloucester, she (literally) fought her way to the throne and in the spring of 1141 Stephen of Blois was defeated and captured. A clerical council elected Matilda as Lady of the English.

The barons though hadn't changed their spots and betrayed Matilda again. This time they sided with Stephen's missus – that was Matilda of Boulogne, not related to our Matilda.

In the autumn of 1141 this Matilda of Boulogne defeated the rightful Matilda's army before the short-time Lady of the English had a chance to be crowned.

In spite of her failure to become the first queen of England, Matilda – a strong and determined broad whom the mob of misogynist barons could not control – has remained in history as the Mother of the Degenerates – the dynasty which, beginning with Henry II, ruled England for more than 330 years from 1154 to 1485.

Oops – my apologies again! I meant to say Matilda has remained in history as the *Mother of the Plantagenets*. Why do I keep making this sort of blunder? Perhaps it's because of my non-English speaking background.

Trivia:

Matilda's eldest son, Henry II, was the first Plantagenet king. It was noted before that Geoffrey Plantagenet (Henry II's pop) was his wife's junior by eleven years.

It so happened that, as his mother had in 1128 married a Frenchman, in 1152, Henry II also married a Frenchman. Sorry, it was a French *woman* he married. And she wasn't any woman; she was the famous Eleanor of Aquitaine, former wife of French King Louis VII. Curiously enough, Henry II was Eleanor's junior by … eleven years.

Another famous royal marriage was that between Mary I of England and Philip II of Spain from 1554 to 1558. Again, Philip was his wife's junior by eleven years!

Eleanor of Aquitaine
(1122 – 1204)

This Eleanor dame wasn't a queen either; she was just queen consort, but consort of two kings. That's not the only reason she also warrants a few paragraphs.

Born in 1122, Eleanor is said to have been of exceptional beauty and had a legendary sense of adventure. At fifteen she married King Louis VII of France who proved to be no match for her extravagant appetite for naughtiness and sex.

Louis was rather a monastic character who, if needed to choose, always attended the Sunday mass while letting a cosy invite from his young wife pass. The broad wasn't happy with her monk-like husband and sought gratification elsewhere.

In 1147 Louis joined the Second Crusade and took Eleanor

with him. A passive dude in the bedroom, Louis was selfish too. Louis knew if he left his missus alone in France, she'd have screwed every man on sight and he thought there was a lesser chance she'd do that in the Holy Land.

Eleanor though proved him wrong. As the Crusaders arrived in Antioch, she began bonking her uncle Raymond, who was seven years her junior. This Raymond was allegedly worldly and virile, and nicknamed Hercules. But not even a Hercules was enough for Eleanor. She wanted More and took a More-ish slave lover. Sorry – that was a *Moorish slave* lover and he became her sex slave.

She finally got tired of slaves and resolved to couple with another king. This time, her plan was to hook up with a masculine king – a requirement which her Louis didn't meet. Eleanor got rid of Louis and one day in 1152 she bumped into the future King Henry II of England.

It was lust at first sight. She thought Henry was her man. Eleanor was self-assured of her presumption because she had in the past checked Henry's pop's credentials and thought that feature was hereditary. They married and had lots of fun.

That's how Eleanor of Aquitaine became the only dame in history to have been both the Queen of France (1137 – 1152) and Queen of England (1154 – 1189).

By Louis VII she had two kids and had another eight with Henry II. Of all of them her favourite was Richard the Lionheart. Like his mother was renowned for, Richard also loved men!

Philogyny and Misanthropy

Just a short digression before continuing with other famous women in English history. We know that misogyny is defined as hatred of women. Though nowadays (particularly in Australia, since the misogyny speech!) misogyny rather implies hatred of women by men, the original definition doesn't differentiate if the misanthropes (the ones who hate) are men or women.

But what about hatred of women by women? Isn't that a more common case than hatred of women by men? I mean, one should hope that worldwide, the more common fashion for men is to love women instead of hating them. This natural inclination could perhaps be described as "reverse misogyny", but I don't think there is such a term as reverse misogyny.

There is however a proper word for love of women and that's "philogyny". Philogyny, being the antonym of misogyny, is defined as fondness, love or admiration towards women. Like in the case of misogyny – where misogynists can be either men or women – the definition of philogyny suggests that philogynists can also be either men or women. Lesbians too.

On the subject of hate, there is a word for people who hate other folks and that word is "misanthrope". A misanthrope is a hater of humankind. I am not aware of a term defining hatred of women by women, though one would think perhaps a word for it should be invented.

I am saying this because there are so many examples! A pertinent one is that the only two queens capitally punished in England were executed by ... two English queens. More, the two queens responsible for the executions – Mary I and Elisabeth I – were half-sisters and were both related to their victims.

First, in 1554 during the reign of Mary I of England, also known as Mary Tudor, or Bloody Mary, Lady Jane Grey was executed and 33 years later, in 1587, Elisabeth I of England oversighted the beheading of Mary Stuart of Scots.

Sure, before that, the infamous Henry VIII, who was also Mary and Elisabeth's pop, had had two of his wives slayed, but the women had never been queens as such in their own right; they had only been what they call queen consorts.

In 1536 Henry VIII decapitated his second wife Anne Boleyn, who was Elisabeth I's mother. And in 1542, the same Henry VIII executed his fifth wife, Catherine Howard, who was no one's mother. Elisabeth I also was no one's mother and was no one herself, as a matter of fact.

Were the above examples sickening cases of fanatical misogyny? Not sure about Mary and Elisabeth, but, as Henry VIII was certainly a womaniser, there seems to be a contradiction that a "Casanova type" of a man like him could go to such extremes as to kill ladies.

But ... maybe not. According to the English Thesaurus, one of the synonyms of the word womaniser is "lady-killer". In Henry VIII's case, it seems that the literal meaning of lady-killer applies.

Mary Tudor
(1516 – 1558; reigned 1553 – 1558)
Lady Jane Grey
(1537 – 1554; reigned for nine days in 1553)

When Henry VIII died in 1547, his feeble son – Edward VI – aged nine at the time, succeeded him to the English throne. An attempt had once been made to marry underage Edward with Mary Stuart, Queen of Scots. If you thought that Edward VI was too infantile to be king aged just nine, Mary Stuart – who was four years Edward's junior – had become Queen of Scotland at the venerable age of ... six days!

Henry VIII's arranged marriage plan failed, which sparked another invasion of Scotland by the bully Poms, but that's another story.

Before we go any further, do you think it was kosher that Edward VI, aged only nine at the time, was installed on the English throne ahead of his elder sisters? How the heck was kid Edward more qualified to be king compared to Mary and Lizzie who were aged thirty and fourteen respectively?

Isn't that another plain example of brazen misogyny? I mean it's obvious that Edward's only additional "qualifications" compared to his sisters' was that he possessed two balls. Mind you, some have suggested that Elisabeth herself owned a ball or two, though the exact number is unclear.

What's even more pathetic is that this anachronistic tradition where royal boys of any age are made kings ahead of older sisters, still applies today.

Wasn't Queen Elisabeth II lucky that her only sibling was younger girl Margaret? Though Margaret was four years junior to Elisabeth, had Maggie been born a male, the Queen would have kissed the royal chair goodbye.

Back to Protestant Edward VI, in 1553 he died of tuberculosis aged fifteen. At his death, his half-sister, Catholic Mary Tudor (pictured above), was hairy and presumptive to the throne.

Gosh – I keep mixing up words! I didn't mean to offend Mary Tudor suggesting that she was bushy or shaggy or hairy. I meant to say that she was heiress presumptive to the throne.

But some didn't see it that way and, driven by fanatical religious beliefs, a certain freaking Duke named Dudley Moore ... Sorry, it wasn't Dudley Moore; it was *Dudley John* or rather *John Dudley, Earl of ...* something. So, this Johnny

Dudley dick had persuaded the dying king to confer his crown to protestant Lady Jane Grey (pictured below) – who was a cousin of Edward.

I am being cranky with Dudley because, if not for his egocentric interests, Lady Jane would still be alive today. I mean ... perhaps she wouldn't be alive today as such, but she could have lived for many more years and would have raised a herd of children. Well, no one could be certain of that per se, but such a scenario would have been a distinct possibility.

But, as it stands now, Jane's death can totally be blamed on Dudley's narcissistic ambitions. The swine had coupled his own son with Jane, his objective being that, should Jane become queen, Johnny himself would have been queen mother. In short, that was the plot, but it failed.

It is also possible that, when Edward nominated Lady Jane Grey to inherit the crown, the teen had been smitten by Jane's beauty. Unlike Mary Tudor – who wasn't a picture – Lady Jane Grey is believed to have been very beautiful.

Though ugly, Mary Tudor did have a valid claim to the crown. Having previously been declared illegitimate and a bastard, for the false accusation that Henry VIII's marriage to Catherine of Aragon (Mary's mother) had been invalid; in 1545 Mary had been restored to her lawful position in the line of succession to the throne.

So, at Edward VI's death in 1553, Lady Jane Grey was proclaimed queen, which she apparently accepted with reluctance and rightly so, because the vast support around the country was for the Catholic Mary Tudor.

Backed by the masses, Mary claimed the crown without bloodshed and vowed to restore the Catholic faith, which she did for a short while, but with causing loads of bloodshed.

Sadly, after only nine days – the shortest reign in English history – Lady Jane Grey relinquished the crown she hadn't wished for in the first place and was beheaded in February 1554, aged only sixteen.

Mary I, or Mary Tudor, remains known in history by the dreadful nickname of Bloody Mary. In my honest judgement, the "Bloody Mary" label given to her is another pathetic case of blatant, unashamed misogyny!

Well ... it is true that, under Mary's reign, there were quite a number of Protestant Tudors executed because of religious reasons. However, the number of slayings during Mary's reign was actually less than 300. Compare that with the executions ordered by her dad, King Henry VIII, and you'll learn that he was responsible for the killing of some 57,000 men and women!

So, why is Mary I dubbed "Bloody Mary" while Henry VIII – guilty for nearly 200 times as many killings – is not styled "Gory Henry", for example?

Well, the obvious answer is because Mary was a woman and even in those times, men had a perverse pleasure of putting women down. That's more than the literal meaning of the expression may suggest!

Anyway, as a tardive punishment, perhaps historians should consider giving Henry VIII a moniker that he would be ashamed of if he were still alive. Something like "Screwy Henry" or "Gothopotamus Henry", or "Fugly Henry", or "Henry the Big Pig"!

Mary Stuart of Scots
(1542 – 1587; reigned 1542 – 1567)
Elisabeth I of England
(1533 – 1603; reigned 1558 – 1603)

As mentioned in the previous section, in 1542 Mary Stuart (portrayed above) became Queen of Scots when she was just six days old. Being a great-granddaughter of Henry VII (Henry VIII's daddy), Mary was next in line to the English throne after all of King Henry VIII's kids would have had their turn.

Henry VIII's brats consisted of only one frail lad – Edward VI – and two lasses – those being Mary I and Elisabeth I.

It seems that, at that very young age, being the Queen of Scotland and having a valid claim to the English throne wasn't enough for Mary Stuart.

Speaking of Scotland, why are all its dwellers known as Scots? Is every one and each of them named Scott? Females included?

In 1548, aged just five, Mary also became the French queen-to-be, having been betrothed to the Dauphin of France – the future King Francis II – and sent to live at the Frogs' Royal Court. There she was well educated and developed a taste for arts, fine food and delicate things. One of those things was delicately-built Francis, whom she married in 1558.

Francis was two years Mary's junior, so at the time of the wedding he was aged fourteen. It seems that, among royals, misogyny, incest and paedophilia were very common themes.

Regrettably, like Edward VI above, Francis II was of fragile constitution and died two years later, in 1560. Come to think of it, at that time the French didn't have a constitution at all.

Aged just seventeen, Mary became a widow.

In 1561 Catholic Mary returned to her Scottish throne, despite Scotland having officially converted to Protestantism. That's when the trouble began. At the time, Catholic and Protestant gangs were bashing each other and Mary was caught in the middle.

In 1565 Mary met her cousin Henry Stuart, styled Lord Darnley and fell madly in love with him because he was very tall. Darnley was Mary's junior by three years.

They married but didn't get along. Though very tall, Darnley turned out to be arrogant and violent and soon after the marriage, his brand-spanking new missus was madly loathing him.

In 1566, in a rage of jealousy, Darnley killed Mary's secretary David Riccio because he thought Mary was having it off with him.

This Riccio was a very talented musician and performer and apparently the queen had asked him to perform other duties as well. It is believed Riccio had done just that and there were rumours that Riccio had actually fathered Mary's son – the future James VI of Scotland and James I of England. So, the king who united the royal dynasties of the 2 two countries may after all have been the brat of a Latino fiddler!

In 1567 Darnley was murdered, the prime suspect being James Hepburn, Earl of Bothwell.

Again, Mary was a widow, but not for very long. Three months after Darnley's passing she married none other than James Hepburn, reinforcing already growing suspicions that she and Hepburn had indeed been involved in Darnley's murder.

(In case you're wondering, there is no evidence that this James Hepburn was related to either Katharine Hepburn or Audrey Hepburn.)

Following Mary's wedding with Darnley's alleged slayer, whatever had been left of her credibility evaporated. In 1567 the poor queen was forced to abdicate in favour of her one-year-old son.

Naively, in 1568, Mary fled to England expecting Cousin Lizzie to help her regain the Scottish throne. But that was the last thing on Elisabeth's mind. Concerned about Mary's potential claim to the English throne, Lizzie placed Mary into custody. And that's where the ex-queen of Scots and Frogs remained for the next nineteen years.

In 1586 Mary was accused of plotting to replace out-of-date Lizzie. She was trialled later the same year, sentenced to death and beheaded in 1587.

While Mary Stuart was being raised and educated at the French Royal Court, in 1558, Elisabeth I (portrayed below) had become Queen of England. A convinced protestant, Lizzie restored the new religion introduced by her idiotic pop – Henry VIII – and strengthened the authority of the Church of England across the country.

Considered one of England's more prominent monarchs, Elisabeth I is also known in history for quite a few rather curious reasons. Though labelled "The Virgin Queen", there have been innumerable rumours about her sexuality and sexual life.

Some of the gossips say that, aged just sixteen, she was made pregnant by her guardian Thomas Seymour, whose name was mentioned earlier in the book.

Thomas was the brother of Henry VIII's third wife, Jane Seymour. After Henry's death, Thomas married Henry's sixth and last wife – that was the freshly-become widow, Catherine Parr.

Like many honourable citizens during those times, in 1549 Thomas Seymour was executed, but that unfortunate event had nothing to do with his alleged seduction of Lizzie. The future queen was shrewd enough to keep any fling with Thomas hushed up.

In addition to Thomas Seymour, Lizzie is also rumoured to have been romantically or just sexually linked to quite a number of creatures – older and younger, more or less noble, eligible or married, straight, bi or gay, authentic blokes or of uncertain sex and so on. Lizzie was quite a creature herself.

The list of her alleged partners included Lord Robert Dudley (who was married), Sir Christopher Hatton, the glorified buccaneer Walter Raleigh, Henry III of Valois (who was half her age and gay) and Henry's even younger brother, Francis – Duke of Anjou and Alencon, who was Lizzie's junior by 22 years and whom she dubbed "my frog". (I'd have thought that was offensive).

From the above list, Henry III of Valois deserves a further remark. Believe it or not, this Merry Henry was King of France from 1574 to 1889. In 1570, when plots to couple him with Queen Elisabeth began, Henry was nineteen and she was thirty-seven.

It seems Henry wasn't too fond of the strange queen. Being a Pommy, she was indeed a stranger in that sense but more than that, she was very strange indeed in the other meaning of the word. No wonder Henry didn't fancy her. I mean even if Henry hadn't been homo (and I say this with humour, not insult), how on Earth would even a straight bloke have copulated with the (by all reports) weirdo queen?

Henry made his feelings quite clear. He called Lizzie a "public whore" and an "old creature with a sore leg". That's pretty heavy stuff. (I'd thought she had two of those, but whether they were limbs or glands or organs ... I am not sure).

So, the plot to mingle Lizzie and Henry failed, which is a pity. As far as I understand it, the compatibility rate between them was 80%. She was a queen; he was a queer. That's four out of five matching score, which isn't too bad.

According to other speculations, Liz may have had a different physical problem (like a very thick thing down there) that acted like a natural chastity belt preventing her from being penetrated. And sure, others suspected her sex itself was indefinite.

Having had Anne Boleyn – his second wife and Elisabeth's mother – executed, in 1536, Henry VIII had declared Lizzie illegitimate and a bastard, just like he'd done with Mary Tudor – his first daughter by Catherine of Aragon elder and sis to Lizzie.

Whether she was illegitimate or not, by killing Mary Stuart in 1587, Elisabeth proved she was indeed a bastard in the other, even less flattering meaning of the word.

In addition to being labelled a bastard, Elisabeth I is remembered in history as the queen who bestowed her name to the American state of Virginia. It is said that Virginia and West Virginia have been named after her, based on the assumption that Liz was The Virgin Queen.

Actually, the process was a little more involved than that. Late in the 16th century, Pom explorers surveying the area around Carolina and Virginia came across a native Indian chief named Vagina and thought that name was appropriate for Lizzie, so they named that region after her.

Hmm … something isn't right here. It looks like I messed it up again. That Indian chief was actually named Wingina, from whinging, not Vagina from … whatever.

So, because Elisabeth was whinging, although already a hoary gaga, she was still a virgin, they branded that district Virginia. Makes sense now?

Trivia:

It is said that Elisabeth was in the habit of drinking two pints of strong beer for breakfast. Wasn't that a royal treat?!

Queen Mary II
(1662 - 1694; reigned 1689 – 1694)
Queen Anne
(1665 – 1714; reigned from 1702 – 1714)

Queen Mary II (pictured above) and Queen Anne were two of the daughters of King James II of England and Ireland and James VII of Scotland. I should perhaps clarify that Mary and Anne were not the daughters of 2 two different kings. What I meant to say is that King James II of England and Ireland was the same dandy as King James VII of Scotland.

Mary and Anne were raised in an exclusively female ménage at Richmond Palace. It was probably natural that, from an early age, the future queens acquired a fondness towards dames and a compulsive liking of a certain sweet tropical fruit. (That's the Lady Fingers variety.)

It is said that aged just twelve, Mary had a crush on a certain Lady Frances Apsley (aged 20), to whom, she later referred to as "my dear husband". She also had a sweet husband.

Anne – Mary's sis – at one stage, also fancied the same Frances and had a love affair with her. It makes you wonder if that was technically incest. Well, I suppose, because in those times, the ladies could not have legally married each other, no one really gave a hoot about it.

Mary, having been brought up as an Anglican, was betrothed to her first cousin, Protestant William Prince of Orange. William was the son of Charles I's daughter – also a Mary Stuart, but another one – not the one we just discussed above.

This other Mary Stuart was Princess of Orange and Countess of Nassau. She was also married to a William of Orange, but another one – not the one who was to wed Mary II.

(Above: Queen Anne)

As Mary Stuart was the elder sis of James II, and James II was Charles I's second son, it works out that James II's daughters were first cousins of William of Orange. Incest has become a rather tedious issue in this book!

And paedophilia too! Mary was sent to Holland where, in 1677, she married Prince William of Orange. He was 27 and Mary just fifteen. It wasn't however a bad match. Mary was a lesbian and William gay, but not in the sense of merry, nor bright in colour either.

In fact, come to think of it, orange is quite a bright colour. Anyway, Mary wasn't impressed with her Flemish. Sorry, William was *Dutch*, not Flemish. What I meant to say was that she wasn't impressed with his blemish. So, she told William off. She also told him to go Dutch. Which they did.

Amazingly, given his preference towards cocks-combs, in 1680 William took a mistress, while Mary found consolation in pleasing Dutch women.

Did I say cocks-combs? Like those things with which you comb your pubic hair? No – I am told. Cocks-combs don't exist yet, but they should be invented for the exclusive use by *coxcombs*.

At the time, Charles II was reigning in England, but in 1685 he resolved it was time to die, so the crown passed to James II. With James II being a Catholic, trouble was imminent at home.

Again, the strife came from the gang of noble Poms, who asked James's son-in-law to travel by sea from Holland to England and depose the Catholic king. In a daring act that remains in history as the "Glorious Revolution", William did just that.

As a little stimulus, Mary had been offered the English crown, but William was thirsty to be queen as well. Sorry, he was queen already, but he wanted also to be king. So, in 1688 Mary II and William III became the only pair of joint monarchs in English history.

In 1694 Mary, aged 32 died of smallpox. After Mary's death William ditched his mistress and resurrected his original vocation to chaps, particularly pageboys.

In 1702 William, by then 51, passed away of pneumonia. He died on the 8th of March – a date which, two centuries later, was to be proclaimed in his honour the "International Woman's Day".

On William III's death the crown passed to Mary's younger sis, Anne who was also a lesbian. Sorry, I meant to say that she was also an *Anglican.*

In 1683 Annie had married Prince George of Denmark. Oddly, Prince George was apparently straight. In the seventeen years from 1683 to 1700 Annie had seventeen pregnancies, but only one of the kids survived infancy. The boy died in 1700, aged eleven.

Depressed by all those tragedies, Annie began to hit the bottle and was later nicknamed by her subjects "Brandy Nan". They probably meant "Annie, Brandy Nannie".

She also grew enormously fat, which may have caused her to appear undesirable to men, but not to women, as one of her famous lovers was Sarah Jennings, whom Annie befriended in 1675, when she was ten and Sarah fifteen. At the same age, Sarah met John Churchill – the famous Duke of Marlborough – whom she married in 1677.

It seems that the marriage wasn't an obstacle in Sarah's love affair with future Queen Anne. Her hubby, as a military chap, was often at war, which gave Sarah plenty of recreational time. Most of that time she spent in Annie's boudoir.

When Annie became queen, she found a new passion in a certain Abigail Hill, whom Sarah strongly disliked and disapproved of. A vicious brawl subsequently erupted between Abigail and Sarah. Eventually Sarah lost the affray and was given a red card being forced to leave the Royal Court.

Apart from this scandalous goss, Queen Anne will always be remembered for the signing during her reign of the historic Acts of Union of 1707, which formalised the union between the women of England and Scotland.

Annie was the last of the Stuart monarchs. She died in 1714 aged 49. Ironically, though she had gone through seventeen pregnancies, on her death, Annie had no heirs. The crown nearly passed to another sheila. That was Sophia of Hanover, granddaughter of King James I.

But, having heard of so much scandal and perversity at the British Royal Court, Sophia elected to die instead of taking the throne. She passed away just a few weeks before she would have become queen. That's how her eldest son ascended to the British throne as King George I.

George I
(1660 – 1727; reigned 1714 – 1727)

Thanks to his eccentricity and depraved life, George I, politely described by some as lazy and unintelligent, deserves a bit of attention, but not in a complimentary way.

George made his 1714 entrance to the British Court in majestic style – in the company of not one, but two mistresses.

One was Ehrengard Melusine von der Schulenburg, Duchess of Kendal, Duchess of Munster, Marchioness of Dungannon, Countess of Dungannon, Baroness of Dundalk, Countess of Feversham and Baroness of Glastonbury and Lady Kracken-Fart. Sorry, I am told that *Lady Kracken-Fart* was not one of her titles. Perhaps it was Lady of the Night?

Apart from her impressive collection of aristocratic titles, Ehrengard is said to have leaped to the eye because of her excessively towering stature. Ehrengard was not only very tall; she was also overly thin and fugly, nicknamed "The Maypole" and "The Castle" as in "The King is in the Castle".

George's other mistress who accompanied him to the British Royal Court was Sophia Charlotte von Kielmansegg, Countess of Darlington and Countess of Leinster. Though Sophia didn't have as many noble titles as Ehrengard and nor was she terribly tall, she compensated those deficiencies by being enormously corpulent. Her nickname was "The Elephant".

It is noted that when George left for England, he took with him the above two mistresses, but left his wife behind at home and imprisoned in a castle. That was another castle, not George's mistress, Ehrengard.

Parenthetically, I learned a while ago that the definition of "mistress" is something between a mister and a mattress.

Perhaps, one would think that, fearing he could potentially be blamed of incest, George was ashamed to show off his wife to his Pommy subjects as she was none other than his first cousin, Sophia, Princess of Celle!

Well, that wasn't the case. I mean Lazy George wasn't ashamed of anything. He did even worse than indulging in sexual activities with a first cousin. One of his lovely mistresses – Sophia Charlotte von Kielmansegg – was his illegitimate half-sis!

George I was certainly a degenerate gaga. He even shared

a lover with his pop! And, on top of the pop, apart from his two mistresses he'd brought with him from Hanover, George also appointed a number of local British talents – and even courtesans of ex kings.

How on Earth did he blabber with them? The fool geezer couldn't even speak the language. Otherwise, the most distinctive features about George were those two very weird mistresses of his – "The Castle" and "The Elephant".

Queen Victoria
(1819 – 1901; reigned 1837 – 1901)

Victoria was just eighteen years old when she became queen. At the time, she was Europe's most eligible young woman and had an army of suitors, of which Prince Albert of Saxe-Coburg was finally the successful candidate. The fact that Albert, or Bertie was Victoria's first cousin goes without saying and no longer surprises anyone.

It is said that, having been besotted by Bertie, it was actually Victoria who proposed to him and they were united in early 1840. In the next seventeen years they had nine children, eight of which she married into royal families, earning Victoria the nickname "Grandmother of Europe".

Though regarded as a model of morality (I wonder why), Vicky wasn't exempt from royal scandals and nor was her hubby, Bertie or his family. Bertie's mummy had an affair with the Court's Jewish chamberlain and there was plenty of goss that the fink was Bertie's real pop, which if correct, would make the prince half-Jew. Whether it's true or not remains still unanswered, but Bertie's strait-laced standards of sexual repression are well documented.

It is said that Vicky's appetite for "jiggy-jiggy" was in contrast to Bertie's, who believed that sex was only necessary for procreation, not for enjoyment. To stimulate her hubby, Vicky apparently decorated the royal boudoir with paintings of male nudes!

Bertie was also an adept of abstinence. That's in regards to women! Oops – maybe I shouldn't have said that. Anyway, once the Queen got pregnant, Prince Bertie would refrain from sex for the full duration of the pregnancy plus three months afterwards – for a total of twelve months. Considering that she went through a total of nine pregnancies, it meant that, during her 21-year marriage, Vicky had to go without it for at least nine good years. It must have driven the Queen crazy!

But Bertie's prudish standards didn't do the prince any good. He died in 1861 from stomach troubles aged only 42. The Queen was of the same age.

Victoria, at first, took Albert's death very badly. She retired from public life and, many thought, she was going nuts. That was until in the mid-1860's when she hooked up with a certain Scottish servant, who had the distinguished name of John Brown.

The Queen and her coffee boy were a good match. He was a giant of a man and she measured four foot eleven inches, or a little under one-and-a-half metres. That is in height. She might have been a bit broader than that.

It is noted that the average height of a man in those times was five feet six inches. That's about 168 centimetres. But anyway, they say size doesn't matter. Though, it seems that a little later in Vicky's life, size suddenly did matter.

Brown was good-mannered too, he talked to the Queen addressing her simply as woman and at times even worse – such as Hey, cow, get your arse over here! But he only did that when he had too many shots. The Scot loved his Scotch! He is said to have been both a sook and a legendary soak.

By talking tough to her, Brown apparently impressed the Queen, becoming her hubby de facto. It was at the time speculated that he made Vicky pregnant and that they secretly married.

After John Brown died in 1883, Vicky converted from legendary queen to unseasoned novelist, writing and publishing a book dedicated to ... John Brown.

Subsequently, from writer she turned into a cougar, but not as in the large cat also known as panther or puma. It is rumoured that in the 1880's the already senile queen had one last fling with Indian Muslim court attendant Munshi Hafir Abdul Karim (another distinguished name!), who was in his twenties. To besot the Queen, this Karim must have had lots of charisma.

When she was warned by the government that her cosy

relationship with a black man was inappropriate, the queen apparently argued that generally speaking, dark-coloured fellas had a particularly desirable talent which most of their pale-skinned counterparts lacked.

While it is obvious from the above paragraph that during those times, Pom politicians needed significant training on the subject of political correctness, Vicky's argument may have been the precursor of the Reverse Racial Discrimination movement (or Reverse Racism), which was launched and flourished in the late 20th century.

We know that in 1877 Victoria had been proclaimed Empress of India. During that time the British Empire did bloody well, reaching its top in terms of size and other stuff. India, as the centre of the empire, was then known as the "Jewel in the Crown". Now, learning of this Indian Karim, I wonder if to the queen, *he* was the Jewel in the Crown.

Queen Victoria died quietly three weeks into year 1901 at the age of 81. For the next 114 years to 2015 she remained in history as Britain's longest serving monarch.

Her absolute record of 63 years, seven months and two days on the throne was surpassed on 9 September 2015 by Queen Elisabeth II.

Elisabeth II
(Born in 1926; reigning since 1952)

The Queen (pictured above) has already been talked about in this book, but, being ... the Queen, she probably deserves a separate section, even if it's a short one. So much has been said and written about Queen Elisabeth II that I couldn't possibly add anything of great interest. I will just ramble a little, so that, in case she reads this book, she won't feel left aside or neglected.

Queen Elisabeth II is the Head of State of the United Kingdom and of a number of other states and territories. I won't attempt to count or list her full titles, nor those states and territories because that would require the filling in of too many pages and readers would get bored stiff going through the register.

I will however mention that her full name is Elisabeth Alexandra Mary Windsor and she is the Queen of the United Kingdom and of 16 sovereign independent states part of the Commonwealth.

Elisabeth is also the head of the State of Australia. She was born on 21 April 1926. We, Australians, celebrate her birthday with a public holiday on the second Monday of June! Why the heck do we do that?

Well, the Queen's grandfather, King George V, was born on the 3rd of June, 1865. So what? One would rightly ask. I once asked myself the same question and was told that the second Monday of June is closer to 3 June than it is to 21 April. Got it? I didn't, but it does make a lot of sense!

Apparently, the Queen is the legal owner of one-sixth of the Earth's land surface! How about that?! According to quite a number of entries on the Internet, she owns some 6,600 million acres of turf, or one sixth of the Earth's land surface. I know I am repeating myself saying this, but I just want to emphasise how big a parcel she owns is.

At about 4,047 square metres in one acre, 6,600 acres translates to a total area of some 26,710,200,000,000 square metres, or 2,671,020,000 hectares, or 26,710,200 square kilometres.

The earth's land area is about 29.2 % of its total size (the remaining 70.8% is water) or, some 148,940,000 square kilometres. One sixth of it (or 16.67%) equates to 24,823,333 square kilometres.

So, if it is true that the Queens owns 6,600 million acres of land or 26,710,200 square kilometres, the actual size of her land holdings is nearly 2,000,000 square kilometres more than one sixth of the Earth's surface area. Or, in other words, the Queen owns 17.93 % of the Earth, rather than 16.67%.

To form an idea of how rich Her Majesty may be, the size of her land holdings is about 110 times larger than the United Kingdom (whose area is 243,610 square kilometres) and some 205 times bigger than England (which is 130,395 square kilometres in size).

Paradoxically, though the legal owner, in practice, the Queen cannot profiteer from her apparent immense wealth – i.e. she cannot flog off even a square metre of her land.

Her personal wealth is estimated at some $550 million US dollars and includes farms and castles, marine lands in England and Scotland, objects of art and jewellery and one of the world's finest stamp collection. Assets belonging to the Crown Estate, such as the Buckingham Palace – valued at around $5 billion US dollars – and the Royal Art Collection are not part of the Queen's personal wealth.

Her annual royal allowance or, in other words, pocket money is $13 million dollars. Well, her steep-end is quite steep! Sorry – I am told it should be referred to as *stipend*, not steep-end. They – that's the British Government – probably determined it as one million per month with an additional million being her "13th salary", or "Christmas Bonus".

Being of Romanian descent, I will proudly end this section mentioning that Queen Elisabeth II is a third cousin of Romania's last king, Michael I or Mihai who reigned from 1927 to 1930 and again from 1940 to 1947, when he was forced to abdicate by the Communists. King Mihai was born in 1921 and is still alive and doing well. The very same Queen Elisabeth II is said to be a descendant of Romanian Voivode Vlad the Impaler, aka the infamous Vlad Dracula!

Princess Margaret, Countess of Snowdon
(1930 – 2002)

Have you ever contemplated that Elisabeth II would not be queen today if not for two milestone events which happened in the 1930's and in which the main protagonists were both women?

I guess I am not exaggerating when asserting that the Queen owes her celebrity status as one of the most famous women in history to two women.

Of course, the third or rather first woman was her mother, and King George VI may also have played a role. But here I am referring to two other women. Not in the sense of "the other woman".

One of the two women was Wallis Simpson who had smitten King Edward VIII to such a degree that, on an early winter day of 1936, he declared something perhaps like: Stuff the British throne! – I don't fancy sitting on it anymore! I wanna sit on something else!

Well, perhaps these were not his exact words, but sure there must have been something to that effect.

He opted to sit on top of Wallis, not that it was much fun for Wallis. She must have felt that this was all the king was doing – just sitting on top of her. No more than that.

Should Edward have put duty before love, his younger brother – George VI (who was Elisabeth's father) – would never have been king and most likely, today, Elisabeth II would not be Elisabeth II, but … just Elisabeth, or perhaps Libby, or Beth, Betty, Lizzy, or Lizette.

The other woman who played a decisive role in the Queen's fortune was none other than her own sister – Princess Margaret, Countess of Snowdon, pictured above.

Had Princess Margaret chosen to be born a boy, though younger than Elisabeth, the lad would have been made king first, denying Elisabeth's ascension to the throne.

It seems that, even from when she was in her mother's womb, Margaret decided that being a sheila was going to be more fun than if she were born a bloke. Most likely, she was right.

As she grew into a young woman it was obvious that Margaret had all the equipment necessary to stir naughty desires in the other gender.

At fourteen Maggie had a huge crush on Captain Peter Townsend who was aged 29. Things went well between Townsend and the young princess, except for the little detail that Maggie's suitor was married and the princess had to wait until he got a divorce.

Struggling with impatience, Maggie began to amuse herself with other young chaps. One not so young was American entertainer Danny Kaye – nineteen years Margaret's senior. It was later revealed that Kaye had had other famous lovers, not necessarily Dames. But at least one of them was the male equivalent of a Dame; that is, a Knight.

(I was staggered to learn that one of Kaye's bed partners was none other than screen legend Laurence Olivier, who in 1947 had been made a Knight.)

Dear me – aren't some of these celebrities absolutely amazing? What's more perplexing is that at the time of his love affair with Kaye, Laurence Olivier was married to Vivien Leigh!

And what a gorgeous woman Vivien was! But not as lovely as Danny Kaye – Olivier obviously deemed. Well … it's a matter of taste after all.

Back to Margaret, she waited and waited … and, when in 1952 Townsend's divorce was finalised, the princess's dream of marrying him nearly came true.

But, as history always tends to repeat itself, the Edward VIII–Wallis Simpson love story did repeat itself. The Pom politicians in alliance with the Church of England refused to allow the marriage to go ahead for the very same reason that Townsend was a divorcee.

Winston Churchill, who earlier had supported Edward VIII to "marry his cutie", was now Prime Minister. This time he changed his tune, opposing Maggie's marriage to Townsend.

Sure, Maggie always had the option to tell both Churchill and the Church to get stuffed, as Edward VIII had done before. Had she chosen to do that, she'd have had to renounce her royal titles and lose the dole she was receiving from the Civil List.

Well, it wasn't the dole as such, but still like a dole. I mean the princess was unemployed and needed charitable assistance – as all royals do – for life. So, losing the dole would have been quite a blow, as the princess was in the habit of spending like a drunken sailor.

Being at that time second in line to the throne, had Margaret decided to defy Churchill and the Church and go ahead with the marriage, she would have lost any potential claim to the British crown. She was definitely mindful that, should she one day be queen, she'd have collected even more dough from the Civil List.

Keeping all that in mind, the princess carefully considered her position and in 1955 she chickened out and kissed beau Townsend goodbye. The captain rushed to Belgium where he married a young local lass who was half his age and looked like she was Maggie's identical twin. That was a smart move. Not only that he never missed Maggie afterwards, but this Belgian mademoiselle was a younger version of Maggie.

Maggie didn't miss the captain either. After despatching him to Belgium, she spent most of her time partying, playing around and hitting the bottle.

She embarked on a number of flings with fops like Billy Wallace, who, just before their planned engagement, took off to the Bahamas where he fell in love with an indigenous bimbo. Well, not that he fell in love per se but he certainly fell in bed with her.

"Good riddance!" said Maggie and continued her wild parties with chaps like Dominic Elliot (son of the Earl of Minto), the Earl of Dalkeith, Mark Bonham Carter and various others.

Extra alleged lovers included Colin Tenant, John Turner and Leslie Hutchinson, who was 30 years older than the princess!

In 1960 she married photographer Antony Armstrong-Jones, whom the Queen, in recognition of his talents, promoted from paparazzo to the title of 1st Earl of Snowdon.

Tony's most notable flair was his flawless impartiality. He equally fancied dames and chaps, though he may have been somewhat deficient in his intimate dealings with ladies.

One strong indication that Tony Arm-strong wasn't such a strong show in the bedroom is that in the mid-sixties Maggie hooked up with another Tony.

This other Tony was a Baritone. Sorry, I meant to say that his name was *Barton* – a good pal of Tony Armstrong. Perhaps Tony Armstrong was such a devoted buddy to Tony Barton that he followed the dictum "what's mine is yours" to the extreme.

(Or, maybe he just needed all the help he could get to settle his conjugal burden. Even if Tony was Arm-strong it seems that he may have also been Micro-soft.)

As her marriage with Armstrong deteriorated, Margaret took more lovers. The very long list included Derek Hart, Lord Lichfield (a cousin of hers who was nine years younger), Robin Douglas-Home, Roddy Llewelyn (seventeen years younger), Aussie cricketer Keith Miller, shady actor and mobster John Bindon (thirteen years younger) and celebrities like Peter Sellers, David Niven (20 years older) and Mick Jagger (thirteen years younger). The princess never discriminated based on age!

Having had so many lovers, by 1978 Maggie was bored to tears with men and finally, divorced hubby Tony. She never married afterwards. Why would she do that? As a single princess, now she could take a truckload of lovers without being accused of adultery.

Thinking of it, I find this Princess Margaret of the 20th century had quite a lot in common with her namesake Margaret de Valois – once Queen of France – whose colourful life is briefly depicted later in this book. Though they lived some 400 years apart, both ladies were gorgeous-looking and always felt the urge to dish out their splendour.

Popes and the Vatican

So far Popes have been mentioned quite a few times in this book. In Europe's history, at times, Popes and kings or emperors were firm allies and at other times, they were at each other's throats.

Why was that? Because in the Middle Ages many of the Popes as well as the kings and emperors strived for absolute power and supremacy.

While Popes claimed complete spiritual authority over all of Christian Europe, the monarchs, on the other hand, demanded political control over the Church within their jurisdictions.

The Holy Roman Emperor deemed it was in his power to appoint and dismiss the Pope, while the Pope demanded that the Emperor be accountable to him and that he, the Pope, was entitled to dispose of the monarch at will. In European history, both situations occurred a number of times.

If this state of affairs doesn't seem to make sense, how about our current constitutional provisions where the Governor General can fire the Prime Minister and the Prime Minister can request the Queen to dismiss the Governor General?

So, in effect, in Australia, the Governor General has the power to sack the Prime Minister and, at the same time, the

Prime Minister can fire the Governor General.

Hypothetically what would happen if the Governor General and the Prime Minister sacked each other at the same time? I am not sure about the constitutional ramifications, but at a practical level, we would probably all be better off!

But seriously, in this ambiguous situation, who is the boss? Hmm ... I think I know the answer. It's always BS – that's not bull ... something; it is Bruce Springsteen!

Anyway, I deviated from the subject. In this brief section, the subject was the Pope, or Popes in general and the Vatican, and no heavy stuff about it; just a few rather trivial things. No talk about spiritual and temporary powers ... sorry, I meant to say *temporal powers.*

But, please be assured, I am not confused; I know that the temporal power of the Popes is ... it's something else than their spiritual and pastoral things. And it's temporary too.

It is (!) – as is everything else in this world. I mean, on Earth, popes may be the closest thing to God, but they are still temporary and have a finite life and an expiry date. Most Popes have a use-by or best-before date too.

Below are a few details about Popes and the Vatican that you may find either noteworthy or if not, for sure uninteresting.

From early in the first millennium, there have been a total of 266 Popes in a period of nearly 2,000 years since St Peter, Prince of the Apostles in year 32 A.D. That means that as at today, the average time a Pope spent on the papal throne is about 7.45 years.

On the question of nationality, there seems to be unanimous agreement that of the total number of 266 Popes, 217 were Italian. There have also been a number of French, Greek, German, Syrian and a few Popes of other ethnic groups.

We know for sure that there has been only one English Pope (Adrian IV in the 12th century), that one Pope was Polish (John Paul II, from 1978 to 2005) and one Argentine – the current Pope Francis. Otherwise, the exact composition by number of the non-Italian Popes is still ambiguous. Nor is it known how many of the Greek Popes were Helen. Well, they all were. I mean not necessarily *Helen*, but surely *Hellenistic*.

The Pope's residence is the sovereign city-state of the Vatican. With an area of 0.44 square kilometres and a population of about 840, the Vatican is the smallest internationally recognised independent state in terms of both size and population. That's not very complimentary to the Pope, who, for hundreds of years, believed and claimed that he was the Supreme Lord on Earth!

But with such a small realm, these days, statistically speaking, the Vatican has 2.27 Popes per square kilometre!

Finally, have you ever wondered who would approve the Pope's resignation, should such an event ever occur?

Before Pope Benedict XVI it was thought that the Pope could resign but only hypothetically as, since he is the Supreme Pontiff, there is no one on Earth above him to accept his resignation. However, on 28 February 2013 Pope Benedict XVI made history becoming the first Pope to resign since Gregory XII in 1415.

So, who accepted the Pope's resignation? The answer has stunned me: no one. The 1983 "Code of Canon Law" mentions papal resignation in Canon 332, where it is stated that: "If it happens that the Roman Pontiff resigns his office, it is required for validity that the resignation is made freely and properly manifested but not that it is accepted by anyone". As simple as that!

I'll end this section with a rhetorical question – are Popes and Cardinals who elect the Popes misogynist? Well, in spite of a medieval legend maintaining that a female Pope Joan once existed, the Catholic Church denies there has ever been a Pope of feminine gender.

So, it looks like the advocates of political correctness have a lot of hard work to do and a long way to go until we'll see a sheila wearing the papal tiara.

Imagine that – a hot sexy bimbo dressed in a mini skirt, with high heels, plenty of lipstick and mascara, wearing the papal tiara! Just like a sort of Miss Universe. Gosh, that would make my day! (Though I will admit any woman in the role would be fine, my wishful thinking aside, equally isn't picky, or shouldn't be.) Nonetheless, it would be quite funny, as I find the joke below!

On a bus, a drunk was reading the newspaper while burping from time to time. A Roman Catholic priest took the seat next to him and was soon disgusted by the smell of alcohol and tobacco coming from the intoxicated man and by his belching.

'Excuse me father,' said the drunk after a while.

'What's up son?' replied the priest forcing himself to be civil.

'Do you know what causes arthritis?' asked the drunk, while letting out another loud burp.

Annoyed, the priest thought for a few seconds and returned, 'Arthritis comes from a depraved lifestyle, like too much spare time doing nothing, taking funny stuff, indiscriminate sex, smoking and excessive drinking.'

The drunk just nodded and continued reading.

A couple of minutes later, feeling ashamed that he'd been so brusque to the man, the priest asked much more gently: 'How long have you had arthritis son?'

'Ah, it's not me. It says in the paper that the Pope has got it,' said the drunk.

Feminine and Masculine Common Nouns

In case you wonder what a common noun, as opposed to a proper noun, has got to do with royalty – it hasn't. There is nothing common about kings or queens, though many of them aren't proper either.

Still, this section is related to the battle of the sexes. Actually the "Battle of the Sexes" title was given to three tennis matches between a male and a female player. That's not what I wanted to talk about in this section either, but a bit of background may be of interest to note.

The first match took place in 1973 between male Yankee Bobby Riggs and female Aussie Margaret Court. Though the sex of the players seems implied in their first name, it is safer to specify. You never know, as we'll see below.

The contest was instigated by Bobby's comment that women's tennis was inferior and that the top woman player couldn't beat him though he was 55 and retired. What a shocking, misogynist and discriminatory comment! And politically incorrect too!

Bobby had been the number-one tennis player in the world in the 1940's. I should probably add that he had been the number-one player in the world in the men's professional tennis competition. He measured five foot seven inches or 170 cm in height.

In 1973 Margaret Court was aged 30 and ranked number-one female tennis player on the planet. At 175 cm, she was by two inches or five centimetres taller than Riggs.

Sadly for ladies, that day of May, the 25 years younger and five centimetres taller Maggie Court (below) couldn't find her way on the tennis court and was categorically thrashed by old fart Bobby 6 – 2, 6 – 1.

Without intending to make a misogynist comment, I guess, in the end, Maggie deserved to lose. In my opinion, this is because these days she is a Minister. I don't mean she's a Politician; she is a Minister of the Church and her views on homosexuality and same sex marriage are utterly and politically incorrect! In other words, she is opposed to blokes marrying chaps and broads wedding sheilas!

Maggie's loss to Bobby incited another former female number one, American Billie Jean King to accept Riggs' challenge. The two of them went head to head in the second Battle of the Sexes match, which took place in September, the same year.

(Above: Billie Jean King showing off her legs)

Billie hadn't turned 30 yet and was shorter than Riggs by a little over two inches or about six centimetres. Billy was still 55 and still measured 170 centimetres, or maybe just a tad less as, in the meantime, he had aged by about four months.

(Above: Billie Jean King with Bobby Riggs)

So, it was Billie against Billy. This time the female Billie routed male Billy 6 – 4, 6 – 3, 6 – 3. The victory was clear and undisputed. What is still unclear is what motivated Billie to beat so hard the crap out of old timer Billy.

It wasn't that she was too ardent to revenge Maggie Court's defeat a few months earlier by the same Billy. 'Why not?' one may ask. Because Billie Jean King wasn't straight and subject of straight criticism by Maggie, for the very same reason that she was a lesbian.

Some say, the obvious reason that Billie Jean King beat Billy Riggs so easily was that she was a King! Actually, in French Jean is a masculine first name. You must have heard for sure of famous French actors Jean Gabin or Jean Marais, though, perhaps Jean Marais is not a good example of a male actor.

Well, I am confused again, because Jean Marais was madly in love with another famous Jean and I was expecting a Jeanne. This other Jean was also French and also, apparently, a male. That was Jean Cocteau – the well-known writer, designer, playwright, artist filmmaker and everything else that wasn't already stated.

Jean Cocteau was also 24 years Jean Marais's senior. In spite of the age difference, the two Jeans had a long and steady relationship that lasted some 26 years, between 1937 (when Marais was just 24) and 1963 (when Cocteau died).

So, in French Jean is masculine and its feminine form is Jeanne. A notorious Jeanne that comes to mind is of course, Jeanne d'Arc – the legendary French heroin who changed the course of the Hundred Years' War, already mentioned in this book.

Actually Jeanne too was also already mentioned earlier in this book, though you may not recall it as she was earlier referred to as Joan of Arc. That's the English version of Jeanne d'Arc, who was also known as "The Mad of Orleans". Sorry, I am told she was nicknamed *"The Maid of Orleans"*.

Thus, the English form of Jeanne is either Joan (as in Joan Collins) or Joanne (as in Joanne Woodward).

Back to the Battle of the Sexes, the third match was played in 1992 between Czech Martina Navratilova and Yankee Jimmy Connors. Martina, also a former number one, was 35 years old and shorter than Jimmy by about four centimetres or less than two inches.

Jimmy was aged 40 and himself a former number one. He won the contest quite easily in straight sets 7 – 5, 6 – 2. Like in the above match, male Jimmy was straight but Martina wasn't.

Anyway, these male and female tennis players are proper nouns and the title of this section suggests I should say something about the gender of common nouns.

Unlike in some other languages, in modern English, nouns identifying non-living objects have no gender. For example, in English, a car is just a car, with no additional connotation as to what gender it may belong. Parenthetically, there are some folks referring to their car as a she, but it doesn't mean the car is a female. It's like calling your MIL (that's mother-in-law) a bomb, which doesn't imply she is a car. But she may well be just ... a bomb.

As a car is neither feminine nor masculine, we can well assume that it is neuter, or of neutral gender, which seems to make some sense. I mean, why would a car be a he or a she?

Some could suggest that, not being either male or female, a car is a hermaphrodite, but I am not so sure about that either, because allegedly, a hermaphrodite is something that has both sexes and (in England at least), a car is sexless.

Mind you, saying that a car is sexless might not be correct either. I am saying this because there is plenty of sex taking place in cars, (particularly on the back seats). But it is also true that this sort of stuff is quite widespread in Romance language countries and maybe not so much in England.

In contrast to English, in other tongues – and this consistently applies in Romance languages – sexless objects are assigned a gender.

Speaking of sexless, I would also note that not all objects are necessarily sexless. Take for example a vibrator – but not those used in bells and buzzers.

So, in French for example, the word for a car is "une voiture", which is a feminine noun. In Spanish, a car is named "un coche" or "un automovil" or "un carro" and is of masculine gender.

In Latin languages, the distinction between nouns of masculine and feminine gender is made by the use of both definite and indefinite articles placed either in front or at the end of the noun.

Perhaps I should add that more often, these rowdy Latinos put other definite articles in front of, or behind nuns. Sorry – I meant to say *nouns*, not *nuns*.

The definite and indefinite articles have separate forms for feminine and masculine nouns. Sure, these articles do have different forms, shapes and sizes.

The rules get even more complicated when dealing with the plural form of nouns. That's when more than one duo is involved.

It is also curious that in different Latin languages, the same objects can be given different or opposite genders (see above – car is feminine in French and masculine in Spanish).

And, if that isn't enough, in Romanian for example (also

a Latin language), in addition to feminine and masculine, common nouns can also be of a neutral gender.

It would seem logical that nouns distinguishing living creatures or beings should be either feminine or masculine and those defining sexless things would be neutral. But someone decided it would be too simple.

So, in Romanian, a car is of feminine gender (called "maşina"), a tree is masculine ("copac") and a ship ("vapor") is neutral. And wait – in Romanian, a synonym for car is "automobil". While a car referred to as a "maşina" is of feminine gender, the same car, when named "automobil" is a neutral noun.

And there is more! Regardless of the car being named masina or automobil, different makes of cars can have different genders. For example, a Mazda, or Toyota, Honda, Kia, Volga, Skoda, Lada, or Dacia (Romanian-made car) is feminine and a Rolls, Bentley, Ferrari, Lamborghini, Fiat, Ford, Chrysler, Volkswagen is neutral.

That is, everything that ends in an "A" is a female, like "angina" for example, though "angina" wasn't exactly the word I had in mind.

We don't have such confusions in English, or … do we? In English, grammatical gender is always the same as natural gender. For example, we have man and woman, boy and girl, uncle and aunt, nephew and niece, bull and cow, dog and bitch, Kevin Rudd and Julia Gillard and so on.

But there are some peculiarities in English as well. I mean, that's in addition of English folks being peculiar. These aren't just some; it's most of them.

One oddity is the noun "ship". Why do we say about a cruiser, for example: "She's a magnificent ship, isn't she?" How come a car is just a car but a ship is, or can be, a she? Is it just because when pronounced, the word "ship" sounds like a "she" with a "P" at the end? But, if I remember well, a "she" usually has a "P" in front.

Another oddity, we made ourselves. Generally speaking, in English nouns defining occupations or professions have no gender. There is only one form for accountant, bookkeeper, librarian, pilot, carpenter, gardener, plumber, electrician, writer, poet, painter, reporter, clerk, typist, assistant, secretary, banker, professor, driver, barber, lawyer, politician, director, president, etc. regardless of one's gender.

There are exceptions though, like waiter and waitress, barman and barmaid, masseur and masseuse, policeman and policewoman, chairman and chairwoman, actor and actress. These feminine forms of nouns are widely accepted and used in the day-to-day communication, except for "actress" which seems not to be fashionable any longer. And I wonder why.

When I arrived in Australia some 30 years ago (incidentally, I come from Romania), we all differentiated, in speech and in writing between male actors and female actresses. When referring to a woman performer we always said "actress". But not anymore. Now, if talking about Kate Blanchet or Nicole Kidman, for example, we refer to them as "actors". Or worse – "female actors".

Why is that? Is it another case of political correctness taken too far? But, even if that's the case, it's contradictory. I mean a lady giving people massages for example, is still called a "masseuse", not a "female masseur", but a woman performing in cinematography is no longer an "actress"; she's just a "female actor", even when she "massages" another actor! I just don't get it.

Don't you think that in addition to being ridiculous, such examples of political correctness taken too far encourage misogyny as well?

If someone decided that men engaged in moviemaking are "actors" while women having the same occupation are to be called "female actors", why didn't they do it the other way around? I mean why don't we say for example that Katie Holmes is an actress and Tom Cruise is a "male actress"?

Trivia:

On the topic of political correctness, I once provoked a colleague well known in the department where we worked for his contempt towards such "nonsense", as he put it when referring to political correctness. Not that I was a supporter of political correctness; I just wanted to test his own convictions.

'Don't you find any positives at all in the ideas and policies which political correctness promoters are trying to make the community aware of in order to improve and eliminate outdated practices?' I asked.

'Nope,' he sternly returned.

'How about being tolerant and broadminded and treating equally other races like African black people for example?' I continued.

'What you mean?' he asked.

'Well, take for example Barack Obama. Who on Earth would have thought maybe 50 years ago or so that one day, the most powerful man in the world would be a black? It has never happened before and no one would have thought it was ever going to happen. But, thanks to broadminded policies like affirmative action and political correctness, he's made it,' I said.

The bloke snorted contemptuously. 'You sooks amaze me with your naivety. These media punks always say this sort of crap that Obama is the most powerful mac in the world and he's the first-time ever black to pull it off and so on. You know what I say to that?'

Curious to hear his answer, I said I didn't know what he'd say to that.

'Well, first, Obama is not the most powerful man in the world. Not even the most powerful gal,' he added laughing rowdily. 'And even if he was, how about Joe Louis some 80 years ago and Sony Liston in the sixties and then Muhammad Ali and Joe Frazier and George Foreman and Ken Norton and Mike Tyson and ...'

'Okay, okay – I got the idea,' I interrupted.

'Weren't those punks the most powerful men in the world? And they were all blacks,' the bloke stressed his point once more.

How could I argue with that?

Men's and Women's First Names

Since ancient times, proper nouns used as the first names of people were intended to identify the gender of the person and this rule has generally worked as envisioned.

There is little doubt that persons with names like Anne, Catherine, Elisabeth, Jane, Margaret, Mary, Matilda or Victoria for example, are women (and some of them were, or still are queens as well), as presumably, people named Alexander, Alfred, George, Charles, Edward, Harry, Henry, James, John, Louis, Richard, Stephen or William are all males. Though these are names of a few of the British kings, it doesn't mean that I am biased towards royalty. If I were, it wouldn't be kings.

Well, strictly speaking, when queens are named Anne or Mary, or kings are Charles, Edward, Richard or James, we don't know for sure if they are male or females. See examples earlier and later in this book.

There are quite a few instances where names given to females are derived from male names and vice versa. No problem with that – it's just a consequence of the affable coexistence between the sexes! Some would even use this argument to dispute that misogyny does indeed exist!

From the above list of male names, we can deduce that

names like Alexandra, Frida, Georgie, Charlotte and presumably Edwina, Henriette, Jacqueline, Joan or Johanna, Lois, or Luisa, Richelle, Stephanie and Wilma have evolved from their corresponding male names.

Though there are fewer converse cases where male names are derived from their female equivalents, Keith probably comes from Catherine or Kate and Victor from Victoria (or, is it the other way around?)

Trivia:

In the early 1800's nearly a quarter of all the women in England were named Mary.

Names like Jan can be males in some Scandinavian and Slavic languages (common in Czech) and females in English. Remember the Yellow Pages ad "Not Happy Jan"? which evolved into common Australian vernacular.

Marian is a male name in Romanian for example, while same Marian can be a lady's name in English. The one example that comes to mind is Lady Marian – the legendary sweetheart of Robin Hood.

The more common Marianne is presumably an extension of Marian. Interestingly enough Marianne is a national symbol of the French Republic – an allegory of freedom and reason, and a depiction of the Goddess of Liberty.

This Marianne of France was apparently "born" during the French Revolution that began in 1789. So, after hundreds of years of Salic Law, when sheilas were not allowed to be kings (and not even queens!) and the Kingdom of France was embodied in masculine figures, the women of France came back with a vengeance. There is the proof – today "France" and "republic" are feminine nouns as are the French nouns for "freedom" and "reason".

Actually it's more than that. We've all read or heard at some stage the slogan of the French Revolution. That's "Liberté, égalité, fraternité", or "Freedom, equality, fraternity".

Well, all these three words – liberté, égalité, fraternité – are feminine nouns in French. Isn't it strange that even "fraternité" which, by definition, refers to something masculine (that is fraternity or brotherhood, as opposed to sisterhood) is in French a feminine noun? Aren't the Frogs perhaps overdoing it a little?!

Liberté • Égalité • Fraternité
RÉPUBLIQUE FRANÇAISE

Back to this Marianne mademoiselle (symbolized above) signifying the Republic of French, she seems to be quite a precise representation not only of the women of France, but of all sheilas around the world. I mean since the First Republic, she's changed her mind so many times. That's why, so far, there have been no less than five French republics!

There are some other more confusing situations where first names are sexually ambiguous, like Angel, Carol, Devin, Jamie, Jo, Jordan, Riley, Stacy or Tracy, but talking about "sexually ambiguous", there are also lots of folks in this world who can be described as such; not only names.

Angel for example, as a spirit, is of masculine gender in the Scripture, but that was a very long time ago … Nowadays girls are apparently commonly named Angel, though I only know of one and that is a fictional character too! It's heroine Angel Marie Parrish from the Australian soap "Home and Away" played by actress (sic!) Melissa George. I wouldn't label Melissa an angel, but she's certainly not sexually ambiguous either!

Carol can be either male or female, though, according to data I found on the Internet, there are apparently 84 times more females named Carol than males.

There have been however two Romanian kings named Carol, which is 50% of all Romanian kings! The Kingdom of Romania, which only lasted from 1881 to 1947, was ruled by just four kings.

In addition to Carol I and Carol II, the other two Romanian kings were named Ferdinand and Mihai. The latter, whom the communists had found to be a pain in the back, was unceremoniously despatched abroad in 1947. This King Mihai of Romania is a great-great-grandson of Queen Victoria and third cousin of Queen Elisabeth II. He is still alive and married with Anne, Princess of Bourbon and Parmesan. Sorry – that's *Princess of Bourbon Parma*.

Jamie, Jordan, Stacy and Tracy are apparently unisex names, also referred to as gender-neutral or androgynous names and commonly used by both males and females.

I actually find the description of "unisex names" is in conflict with the meaning of the word "uni", which is defined as consisting of, relating to, or having "only one". Thus, "uni" implies unique or exclusive, which is in complete disagreement with the assertion that unisex names apply to both males and females.

There are also first names that may seem ambiguous, but this is because many of these are abbreviations of longer names. Such are Alex from either Alexander or Alexandra, Cass from Cassidy or Cassandra, Chris from Christian or Christine, Danny from Daniel or Danielle, Jess from Jessie or Jessica, Max from Maximilian or Maxine, Pat from Patrick or Patricia, Sam from Samuel or Samantha and many others.

Mel is an interesting one, being normally a first name for women derived from Melanie, Melinda, Melissa or Melody. But what about the renowned male actors Mel Brooks and Mel Gibson? Are they perhaps a case of male actresses? It's definitely a fashionable trend for boys to borrow names from girls and, even more so, the other way around.

Some other first names sound the same and, if not for the spelling, we wouldn't know if they are meant for boys or girls. We've just spoken above about the male Billy Riggs and female Billie Jean King, but perhaps this is not a good example as the assumed feminine name Billie may at times actually have been a male name too.

Another example is Robin versus Robyn as Robin with an "I" is generally a male's designation while Robyn spelled with a "Y" is most of the time a woman's name. Is that perhaps a hint to remind us that generally speaking, men stress on "I" and women ask themselves "Y"?

And then with Billie and Billy it's the other way around.

Napoleon Bonaparte (1769 – 1821)

As Napoleon's name is mentioned a little later in the book, it would be unfair to his memory not to elaborate a little on his life and military career. I did just that, in the form of a humoristic essay below.

At the turn of the eighteenth century historians can say without being too far off the mark that the vast country of France identified itself with a little clever dick named Napoleon Bonaparte.

Napoleon was born in 1769 in Corsica. At birth he came into this world dressed in a corsage. As a little child, Napoleon was an extremely bright man. At fifteen, he was ranked forty-two out of forty-eight in his class.

As an infant, he always dreamed of making a career in the Army – more precisely, in the infantry. He ended up fulfilling his dream in 1785, when he joined an artillery regiment. In 1793, at the age of only twenty-four, he was made a brigadier general. A little later, he was promoted to the rank of captain and then … just officer.

At that time, the French revolution was in full swing. A lawyer, who had named himself Maximilien Robespierre, was in charge of the hostilities. This man was bad, very bad and also a serial killer. In the 1790's he slaughtered to death all his enemies, friends and family.

Robespierre actually guillotined everyone in the beautiful Kingdom of France. When there was absolutely no one left alive in the whole country, Robespierre was then beheaded by the ones who were still alive.

Napoleon was very small – when he was small. As a grown up man, he was … well, at 169 centimetres, he was quite small. Yet Napoleon was able to compensate for his physical disabilities through a wide range of intellectual deficiencies.

In 1804 he was made emperor. And it wasn't the Pope who named him emperor; it was that deaf-mute musician who was infatuated with Napoleon and had composed many songs, ballads, poems and anthems in his honour. The most famous of these was the Heroic Sonnet of Fate.

Sorry, it looks like I messed it up again. I am told there is no such thing as the Heroic Sonnet of Fate. Perhaps I was confusing it with the *Heroic (Eroica) Symphony* and with the Fate Symphony and … with whatever sonnet.

Impressed and encouraged by that ode, the little corporal went to war against Austria and England and Prussia and …

with everyone else, for that matter – even with his first wife Josephine, whom he divorced in 1809.

He soon conquered all Europe, but not all of it. He did however conquer the daughter of Austria's Emperor, whom he married in 1810. I mean, Napoleon didn't marry Austria's Emperor; he married the Emperor's daughter, Maria Louisa.

Napoleon's downfall came when he unwisely decided to invade Russia at the time when Russia wasn't yet the Soviet Union, but still, it was very big and large and very cold, but not as cold as was the Soviet Union during the Cold War.

Napoleon apparently hadn't learned from history's lessons – specifically from Hitler's disastrous campaign in Russia some hundred and thirty years later.

So, he ignored repeated warnings from the Weather Bureau and underestimated the long, cold Russian winter, which was very cold in winter. The French army left for Russia in high spirits, but only lightly dressed. The French soldiers proved to be no match for the Russian bears. It was freezing cold and it all ended up very sad.

In Europe, the period from the mid to the end of the eighteenth century witnessed a strong movement of various feminist movements, including women's rights, liberation and emancipation. It's what we today call feminism.

At that time, Maria Tereza was reigning over Austria. She also owned a big chunk of the Balkans. In Russia, it was Catherine the Great who called the shots.

So, in as early as the 18th century, women who might have complained of being unfairly targeted by misogynists or felt discriminated against were finally vindicated. I mean, two of the most powerful countries in Europe were led by broads.

Catherine of Russia was very proud and ambitious and very sensitive too. She loved animals, particularly horses.

(Above Left: Maria Tereza of Austria)
(Above Right: Catherine the Great of Russia)

Both Catherine and Maria (as in Tereza) also loved Poland. As a matter of fact, in 1772, the two floozies divided Poland between themselves into two equal halves, of which Catherine took the larger half. The third half was given to Friedrich the Great who was then the boss of Russia. Sorry, Friedrich had a P in front; so it was Prussia he was the chief of. Actually, Catherine also had a P in front, but she was only in charge of Russia. But I shouldn't say *only*, as Russia was always much larger than Prussia.

After Maria and Tereza passed away, Catherine remained a single widow. And, perhaps being a little bored, she again divided Poland – twice in fact. There was a hint at the time that nothing was ever enough to satisfy Catherine.

One of Maria Tereza's countless children was Marie Antoinette, who became the King of France when she married the heir to the royal throne. In case you wonder why I just referred to Marie Antoinette as the King of France, I am reminding you that in France, the Salic Succession Law did not permit women to accede to the throne, which means she couldn't have been queen.

(Above: Marie Antoinette)

Marie's queen was Louis ... something. (Why were they all named Louis? And there were eighteen of them altogether. That's only in France. Sort of boring, isn't it? Why not name them Ludovic, for example? Sorry – I am told that Ludovic and Louis is the same name in different languages. Well ... it's still boring.)

Marie Antoinette was also decapitated; by the same Robespierre monster mentioned above and named ... Robespierre. At her death, all of Europe's monarchs grieved and shed plenty of tears. The other kings and queens just laughed and had a ball. Some of the kings had two balls.

Napoleon Bonaparte was killed in battle, at Leipzig in 1813. Well, perhaps that's not strictly accurate, but he was morally killed. He also died at Waterloo in 1815 and again, six years later, in the island of Saint Helen. His memory however will always remain with us untarnished and live.

Kings Who Loved Men

Are Greeks misogynist? If you thought this query came out of the blue, it is a leading question. I mean it's a question that leads me to start this bit of the book with an assorted gag (which I meant only as a laugh, not intending to antagonise anyone).

A Greek and an Italian were arguing, 'We are the greatest,' said the Greek. 'We've had Herodotus, Aristotle, Pythagoras and Alexander the Great.' 'And we had Julius Caesar, Dante Alighieri, Michelangelo Buonarroti and Leonardo da Vinci,' returned the Italian. 'We built the Acropolis, the Parthenon and the Temple of Zeus,' added the Greek. 'We built the Colosseum, the Tower of Pisa and the Piazza of San Marco,' countered the Italian. 'We were the ones who discovered sex,' boasted the Greek. 'That's true,' conceded the Italian. 'But we introduced it to women.'

But seriously, is misogyny akin to homosexuality? Oops, I probably shouldn't use this word – I suspect homosexual may not be a politically correct expression. If I remember well, gay is actually the term preferred over others, but if I used the word "gay", it means other things as well. Or perhaps, under new politically correct guidelines, gay only means … gay.

Paradoxically, I recently learned that the use of the word gay to mean homosexual is actually older than the use of the idiom homosexual to mean gay.

Anyway, there was a brief section earlier in this book about a couple of lesbian queens, so to be fair there should be a few paragraphs about lesbian kings as well. Oops, again! Is there such a thing as *"lesbian male"*? Some think there is.

Seemingly, a lesbian male is a heterosexual man who dreams he had been born a woman, though, even if he were a sheila, she would only make love to other sheilas and never with a bloke. You think it makes sense? Well ... it sure does.

On the subject of gay kings, the first one we know of in English history was William II Rufus (born in about 1056; reigned from 1087 to 1100).

William II Rufus

Rufus – the third son of William I the Conqueror – was known as the Red King because of his rude complexion. Sorry – that should read *ruddy complexion*. His mother was Matilda of Flanders and apparently he also had a sis named Matilda. (There were so many Matildas in those days!)

Apart from the fact that he was ... king, there isn't a lot to say about Rufus. His queens were described as effeminate young men .... Sorry – I should rephrase that. His Court was described as being filled by effeminate young men dressed in extravagant clothes.

During the Red King's reign, the First Crusade was launched by Pope Turban II. Sorry – it was *Pope Urban II* who instigated the First Crusade against the Turbans.

Rufus wasn't drawn into fighting the Turbans. He'd rather battle his brother Robbie, home and away – in England and France. But Robbie did go to the Holy Land, so, as he was missing his wrestling partner; Rufus took up hunting as a hobby. Regrettably, it was an unfortunate diversion. Rufus was killed in a hunting accident, which allegedly wasn't accidental.

William II Rufus never married and he produced no kids. It would have been very weird.

Chronologically, next was gay icon Richard I the Lionheart (born in 1157, reigned from 1189 to 1199). Tall, powerfully built and hugely courageous, Richard was a perfect athlete – the prototype of a superman and great hero of the Third Crusade.

Richard I The Lionheart

In 1191 Richard wedded Berengaria of Navarre – a lovely Spanish Princess – but no one knew exactly why he married her. The king spent most of his time away from home fighting in the Holy Land in the company of a huge herd of young lads, while at home the lonely queen consort was getting sad and felt neglected.

She might have taken the desperate step to complain to the Pope himself of her loneliness, but the Pontiff couldn't help her with that. However, when Richard briefly returned home, the Pope ordered him to fulfil his conjugal duties, which the king pledged to do.

He took Berengaria to church every week thereafter! Slanderous tongues say that the marriage was never consummated. Perhaps the king was just shy to comply with the Pope's request in front of the whole congregation.

The fact that Richard I adored blokes is not a shocker to anyone. But the story that he shared his bed with King Philip II of France is a bombshell.

I had never heard before that Philip II of France was fond of men. And … I don't know anymore. Having done some research, I found that Philip divorced his second wife – Danish Princess Ingeborg – on the grounds that the marriage had not been consummated.

His claim may be questionable, as Ingeborg disagreed, saying that he had, many times, vigorously screwed her, but perhaps the two of them had different ideas about what screwing meant. But, even if Ingeborg was right, this story dating back to 1187 with Philip sharing the same bed with gay Lionheart sounds very suss to me.

Now, one of Lionheart's biographers maintains that Richard's ostentatious bed-sharing with the French king was the product of a political alliance rather than a lovers' tryst and the lurid 1187 act was justified as a symbol of unity between England and France. Well, if you believe that, you also believe that pigs fly.

England's most notorious gay king was Edward II portrayed below. Born in 1284, and reigning from 1307 to 1327, he was already mentioned earlier in the book.

Edward II

Ostensibly, Edward was handsome, generous, smart and loyal. But, during those times, the king's loyalty to male lovers wasn't viewed as an essential royal requirement, and not even as a desirable one at the Royal Court. On the contrary, the barons took repugnance at his openly displayed preference towards pretty boys.

To make things even worse, Edward banned women from the Royal Court! (Well, he wasn't very diplomatic – was he?)

Can you detect any hint of misogyny here? Imagine that today! The male Prime Minister of the country forbidding lady MP's from attending Parliament! Sure, a PM and a king is not the same thing and nor is a Royal Court and a Parliament, but you get the idea.

Should these days a male Head of Government ever dare to do so, the Green ladies in the House would go absolutely ballistic and the Third World War would be on its way.

But Edward II wasn't concerned about Green ladies. In fact, he wasn't concerned about any ladies, be they green or whatever inflections.

Trivia:

Even if it was so long ago, it still seems incredible that such acts of sheer discrimination against women could ever have happened. But how about a relatively recent case involving a very high-profile female scientist?

Madame Marie Curie, who discovered radium and won the Nobel Prize twice, rightly applied for membership to the French Academy of Sciences, but was rejected because she was a woman! It happened about a hundred years ago. Ironically, Marie Curie, who had discovered radium, died in 1934 of radiation poisoning.

Back to men-loving kings, a prominent one was James I of England. This James I of England, born in 1566, was the same bloke as James VI of Scotland, who reigned in Scotland from 1567 to 1625 and in England from 1603 to 1625.

James I

James was brought up in an all-male Royal Court, which could have influenced his sexual orientation. Aged just thirteen, James fell in love with a cousin of his, who was 24 years his senior. Nothing unusual among royals to fall in love with a cousin, nor the age difference, but this cousin of James was a man. He had been well educated and trained at the French Court of (gay) King Henry III.

(Above: James I of England [James VI of Scotland])

Marriage was however royal duty, so, in 1589, at the age of 23, James wed Princess Anne of Denmark, who was fourteen years old. I'm no longer surprised. Having learned of so many cases of "babe in arms" royals being married, fourteen seems quite an established age for those times.

In spite of marrying a woman, James's sexual preference towards the same gender persisted. After becoming King of England, James met a handsome lad named James Hay and fell instantly for him. It has been well documented that from 1603 onwards King James and pal James Hay spent plenty of time together "rolling in the Hay".

Already in his late thirties, James I started to really enjoy it. After getting tired of Hay, he learned that variety was the spice of life and subsequently took a crowd of lovers. With first names like Philip, Robert or George, it is very unlikely that any of them was a sheila.

James's son, Charles I (pictured below, born in 1600; reigned from 1625 to 1649), is said to have been narcissistic and effeminate. And on matters of love and sex, Charles had the same inclinations as his old man. In fact, once James kicked the bucket in 1625, Charles immediately began a passionate affair with James's last documented lover, whom he secretly adored. That was George Villiers, 1st Duke of Buckingham, or to Charles, just "sweetheart George".

Charles I

Charles too had to fulfil his royal duties and so he did by marrying Henrietta Maria of France shortly after his ascension to the throne. Daughter of the first Bourbon King, Henry IV of France, when she married Charles, Henrietta was already fifteen – quite a venerable age at the time.

It is said that in the bedroom, things between Charles and Henrietta were not going well. George – Charles' sweetheart – came to the rescue. Not that he replaced the king in the boudoir, but, hey – listen to this – in the meantime, George had taken a mistress; and it was a woman too!

Even more scandalous, this woman – Lucy Hay, styled

Lady Carlisle – was married to James I's former gay lover – James Hay! If that's not enough, at the time of seducing Lucy, sweet George was also married. Blimey! These aristocrats are absolutely pathetic!

When George's wife discovered that her husband was servicing Lucy, she conspired to pass Lucy on to King Charles – a proposal which he refused.

Lucy was well known for being a first-class variety, but the king wasn't the type to show interest in superb dames, nor indeed in any dames.

So, Charles rejected femme fatale Lucy (who apparently inspired Milady's character in Alexander Dumas' famous novel "The Three Musketeers"), but made her a Lady of the Bedchamber.

In that role, the very experienced Lady Carlisle – alias Lucy Hay – educated young Henrietta Maria in the art of seduction. Within weeks, the young queen was pregnant. Whether by Charles or not, who knows? But officially, they had nine children together.

Sure, there have been other cases in the British history, more or less publicised. It was mentioned earlier in the book that Queen Victoria decorated her royal bedroom with paintings of naked men to stimulate her hubby into having fun. Hmm ... I'm not so sure about Prince Albert either.

And even the current consort of the Queen is rumoured to have had such predilections. But no wonder – he is a Greek after all! Such an allusion is supposed to be just a comical reference to the above joke on Italians and Greeks, but maybe it's only amusing for Italians and not quite so for Greeks. Well, it's only a tease and I hope readers of Hellenistic origin will take it as such.

Then again … how about Hellenistic? Why are Greeks as a people and nation identified in reference to a woman's name? And who is this Helen Mother of Greeks from which the Hellenistic word was derived anyway? If it is Helen of Troy, the legend says she was a daughter of Zeus.

The legend also says that at her time, this Helen lass was the most beautiful woman in the world. But even so, Greek lads still found men more appealing! I just don't get it. So, if this Helen of Troy was an offspring of Zeus, why didn't Zeus eat her as he had eaten his wife and sister Metis? It would have prevented the Trojan War from happening and saved a whole heap of strife that went with the war. But I'd better not go into that.

Actress Diane Kruger (above) played Helen of Troy in the 2003 movie with the same name. Sorry – as hard as I tried, I could not locate anywhere on the Internet an authentic representation of Helen of Troy, like a painting, a photo or a hologram, perhaps.

It looks like during those times – some 3,200years ago – Trojans and Greeks were fully equipped for war but didn't pay adequate attention to photograph taking devices. Even a pretty basic mobile phone could have done the job!

Back to the Queen's consort, aka Prince Philip, Duke of Edinburgh – he was born in 1921 and is still going strong.

What raised some eyebrows about the prince's sexual affinities was his 1956 five-month cruise around the world in the company of his personal assistant – Commander Michael Parker (no relation to Camilla Parker Bowles) – whom the prince had befriended a long way back during the war in the 1940's.

There is nothing wrong with a friendship between two men, most of us would argue, but, if everything was cool, why did Parker's wife sue for divorce right at the time of her husband's wanderings on the seven seas in the prince's company?

Not knowing the answer to this potentially indecent question, I'll end this somewhat unconventional section of the book with another joke:

Russian president Vladimir Putin was chatting with his Prime Minister Dmitry Medvedev. 'How about we spend the weekend at the sauna?' suggested Putin. 'Sounds good,' nodded Medvedev. 'We take a couple of young ladies, have a few vodkas, enjoy the sauna and then we have sex,' continued Putin. 'In front of the ladies?!' asked perplexed Medvedev.

Queen Margot of France
(1553 – 1615)

French King Henry IV's name was just cited in the above section. Henry IV was a great king, but it's not him I am still fascinated about; it is rather his very colourful first wife – Margaret of Valois, better known as Margaret of France or Queen Margot.v

As a brief background, Henry was born in France in 1553. In that very same year, across the English Channel, Edward VI of England – follower of the Protestant religion, earlier established in England by his father, King Henry VIII – passed away.

Lady Jane Grey followed Edward as queen but only for nine days and, on Jane's abdication, Bloody Mary – daughter of the same Henry VIII – acceded to the throne and reintroduced Catholicism.

What I found interesting about Henry IV was his ambiguous standing on the markedly important issue at the time, which was religious faith. It is pertinent to note that:

- Henry was baptised as a Catholic.

- He was raised in the Calvinist Protestant faith.

- In 1572, Protestant Henry married Catholic Margaret de Valois (Queen Margot).

- In 1589 Protestant Henry became King of France – a country with a largely Catholic population.

- After becoming King of France, he waged a long war against Catholics trying to establish his legitimacy and impose Protestantism in a mostly Catholic country.

- In 1593, though he had previously declared on several occasions that he would never embrace Catholicism, Henry did just that – he adopted Catholicism.

- in 1598 he issued the Edict of Nantes, granting religious freedom to Protestants.

- in 1599 Henry married his second wife, Catholic Marie de Medici.

So, in 1593, after a four-year war against the Catholics League, Henry permanently renounced Protestantism and joined the Catholic Church! It tells you a lot about his convictions!

Ironically, in 1610 reformed Catholic Henry was assassinated by a Catholic fanatic. Had he remained a Calvinist, it probably would have been a Calvinist fundamentalist who'd have killed him.

Henry IV was nicknamed "The Good King Henry" because ... he was a good king. Most of his numerous mistresses testified he was good. At the time, Henry was also known as "The Green Gallant" because of his numerous mistresses he incessantly entertained.

Seemingly, "The Green Gallant" label was like a synonym for "The Old Playboy". What old playboy has got to do with the adjective "green" I don't really know.

I'd thought "green" rather implies callow, young, immature, naïve, unexperienced, untrained and so on.

Anyway, if one thinks that Henry IV of France was a bit of a "lady-killer" … well, he apparently was, but not quite in the same class as his first wife – Margaret de Valois, or Princess Marguerite, better known as Queen Margot. Not that Margot was a lady-killer; she was rather a "man-eater".

Margot (pictured above), also born in 1553, just a few months before her future hubby, was the daughter of French King Henry II and Catherine de Medici. Her siblings (and there were nine of them) included Francis II, King of France briefly married to Mary Stuart of Scots, Elisabeth of Valois, who married King Phillip II of Spain, Charles IX King of France, Henry III King of France, and Francis, Duke of Alencon – one of the presumed lovers of Queen Elisabeth I of England.

That was quite an illustrious family and, Margot herself was prominent too. It is said that, as a young woman, Margot was famous for her beauty and sensuality, even described by some as "sexually magnetic". Parenthetically, the picture above doesn't seem to substantiate that description. Anyway, whatever magnetism Margot possessed, she seems to have made the most of it.

In history, Margot is best known for being a scandalously unfaithful wife and having a troop of lovers, both during her time as Henry IV's wife (1572 – 1599) and after the marriage was annulled.

Apparently, Margot – a philanthropic character – was a promoter of the idea that "good things need to be shared". And gosh, she was good!

Some of Margot's better known lovers included Henry de Guise, Louis de Bussy d'Amboise, Joseph Boniface de La Molle, the Vicomte de Turenne, Harlay de Champvallon, d'Aubiac, de Saint-Luc, Vermont and Dat de Saint-Julien.

Certainly, Margot was not a misogynist. Believing that women and men should be treated equally, she apparently also had a lesbian affair with a lady-in-waiting!

Though the same can't be said about hubby Henry IV. The King was both misogynist and discriminatory! Despite his womanising ways, he took offence at Margot's licentious life-style and, in 1586, plotted to have her locked up in gentle confinement in a castle, where she remained semi-captive for the next eighteen years.

Strictly speaking, it was Margot's own brother – King Henry III – who imprisoned her, but that doesn't make Henry IV any better. I mean Henry III was still a man and still a Henry. As far as I can see, both Henrys were disgusting misogynist pigs!

And what a waste of talent these Henry swine have caused! Imagine such a gorgeous woman sitting idle for eighteen years locked-up in a castle! Well, she wasn't really idle. Though in detention, Margot is said to even have seduced her warden! That was the Marquis de Canillac.

But what a nut this Henry IV was! If he was so concerned that, while he was screwing half of the country's female population; his woman should abstain from bonking, why didn't he fit her with a chastity belt?

I'll finish this part about Margot and Henry with another gag:

Before leaving on the crusade the knight called the palace's blacksmith and told him to fit a chastity belt to his missus. Having done the job, the blacksmith asked, 'Should I fit her a muzzle as well?'

Trivia:

This Margot doll was a sort of cross between the Houses of Valois and de Medici. Her pop was Henry II of Valois and her mama Catherine de Medici. When Henry IV finally divorced Margot in 1599 he married another de Medici! That was Marie de Medici – a relative of Margot. Compared to Margot, this Marie was nothing short of a saint. Sorry – I should say *Saint Tess*. No! – I am told. There isn't such a thing as a Saint Tess. I see – I got it this time. It should be a *saintess*.

MILS

I only recently found out that "MIL" is an abbreviation standing for mother-in-law. More commonly, MIL is defined as a "very tiny unit". A MIL is apparently one thousandth of an inch and also, one millilitre, or a unit of volume equal to a cubic centimetre.

While I certainly agree that a MIL is a unit of volume, I am not so sure about a very tiny unit or a cubic centimetre. From my experience, a MIL is usually a large unit! Anyway, there are so many things you learn on the Internet these days!

Now, incidentally speaking, when saying that MIL is an abbreviation standing for mother-in-law, one may well ask the question – who on Earth is ever standing for mothers-in-law?

But seriously, is there a link between misogyny and the anecdotal hatred of mothers-in-law? By definition, MILS are women and typically, this hatred of MILS is attributed to men.

I should hope that any pretended hatred of MILS has nothing to do with misogyny and further, I would dispute that such resentment by men towards MILS even exists.

This assertion should perhaps be rephrased by saying that if present, bitterness towards MILS is equally displayed by both men and women. In support of my claim I can assure the reader I have seen and heard quite a few very bad citations about MILS. Such quotes were evenly attributed to both men and women.

One said: *"I detest my MIL. Feeling is quite mutual. She is an evil, nasty, mean, miserable woman and I cannot stand to be in the same room as her"*.

Gee! That's absolutely horrible! I mean the quote, not the MIL.

But, if I said the above excerpt was horrible, how about this one? *"She is a joke – a lying, thieving, controlling, manipulative, fake joke"*.

Another said: *"What she's done goes way beyond mental illness. Mental illness does not make a person evil and my MIL is evil"*.

That's not very complimentary either.

And there are a few more extracts from the Internet below to which I wouldn't even dare to comment.

"Just the mere mention of her name is stomach-turning."

"My MIL makes my skin crawl. She is honestly the most vindictive, controlling, nastiest person I've ever met. She's seriously just twisted."

"My MIL is an evil disgusting piece of trash."

How about this sort of language?! That's pretty heavy stuff! Not even politicians in the Australian Parliament talk so nasty to each other!

Well, sure one of the (female) "Greenies" once called the

(male) Prime Minister a creep, but, one would hope, that has been just a momentary slip of the tongue.

Anyway, let's end the quotes with a nice, flattering one – and one that is also more credible. *"I absolutely adore my mother in law. I am also a size zero and I fart rainbows."*

Now, before going any further, I need to assure you that the anagram below has nothing to do with misogyny either. And it wasn't me who invented it.

It just … happens that using the very same letters, the compound word mother-in-law is an anagram of "Hitler woman". So, compared to a "Hitler woman", MIL is not such a bad substitute for mother-in-law, after all!

And hey! If Hitler is considered the peak of bad and evil, please don't forget: he was a man!

Well … perhaps he was half a man. According to more recent evidence, the Fuhrer suffered from a rare disorder called "monorchism".

Monorchism has nothing to do with monarchy or kings and queens. It is the condition of having only one testicle. It is said that Napoleon Bonaparte had it too.

Trivia:

Pommy King Ethelred the Unready (born in about 968; reigned twice from 978 to 1013 and from 1014 to 1016) allegedly spent his wedding night in bed with his wife and his mother-in-law!

It makes you wonder if both ladies had a go at him that night and if so, was it at the same time or did they take turns?

Most honourable citizens would find any trio of this kind too kinky, but a threesome with a dupe, his bride and her freaking mother would certainly take the crown!

Well, poor fella was already the holder of the crown, but his sweet mother-in-law relaxing in bed with him on his wedding night must have been an even more precious trophy.

This story about King Ethelred the Unready is so incredible! It could be just a legend or an anecdote, if not a joke. Whether it's true or not, it gave me an idea. How about ending this MILS section with a few assorted jokes?

Jokes with MILS

I'll start with this one: Behind every successful man there is a mother-in-law telling him he's a failure. No – I am told this is not a joke. Luckily it's not my case, anyway, or … maybe only half of it. I mean I have never been successful at anything and my mother-in-law keeps reminding me that.

Let's try a "Question and Answer" one.

Question: *What is the maximum penalty for bigamy?*

Answer: *Two mothers-in-law.*

If there is anything a mother-in-law doesn't know, she imagines it.

I've just got back from a pleasure trip. I drove my mother-in-law to the airport.

'How do we know Adam lived in paradise?' asked the primary school teacher. *'He had no mother-in-law,'* replied little Jimmy.

A tramp called the other day and my mother-in-law answered the door. *'Any used beer bottles madam?'* he asked joyfully.

'Do I look like the type who drinks beer?' she snarled back. *'Any old vinegar bottles?'* the tramp rephrased his question.

There was this fellow who saw a sign saying *"Keep your Country beautiful."* He went home and shot his mother-in-law.

Two old ladies were talking. *'I always thought you couldn't stand him. Why on earth did you allow your daughter to marry him?'* asked one of the ladies. *'It's absolutely true I can't stand him,'* admitted the other. *'I just wanted to be his mother-in-law for a while.'*

Two blokes were chatting. *'My mother-in-law has just eloped with my best friend,'* said one.

'Is that right? And who the lucky fella?' asked the other laughingly. *'I have no idea. I have never met the bloke.'*

I am not saying my mother-in-law is tough but when she eats sardines she doesn't bother to open the tin.

My mother-in-law says I am effeminate. Compared to her, I probably am.

What a remarkable woman my mother-in-law is! At 91 years old she never uses glasses. She drinks straight from the bottle.

I yesterday confessed to the psychiatrist that my mother-in-law keeps blowing smoke rings through her nose when she talks to me. It scares the hell out of me. The doctor smiled indulgently. *'You shouldn't worry about something as petty as that,'* he said. *'There are loads of people who blow rings when they smoke.'* *'But that's the whole point,'* I emphasised. *'She doesn't smoke.'*

A woman reported the disappearance of her husband to the police. *'Is there any message you'd like to give your husband if we find him?'* asked the sergeant on duty. *'Yes, please,'* she replied. *'Tell him that mum didn't arrive after all.'*

After my mother-in-law had vanished from home for over a month, I tried to give her description to the police but they just wouldn't believe me.

My mother-in-law was abducted last week. We got a note from the kidnappers saying that, if we didn't pay the ransom, they would send her back.

Max took his mother-in-law to a lush beach resort last year. They had a lot of fun on the beach playing and burying each other in the sand. This year he's planning to go back to the beach and dig her up.

My missus and I have been arguing for months. I yesterday decided it was time to settle it once and for all.

'Your mother has now been living with us for six years,' I reminded her. *'And she's driving me absolutely nuts. I just can't stand it any longer! It's time she moved out and left us alone. It's either her or me!'* I threatened.

My wife stared at me amazed. *'My mother?'* she screamed. *'I thought she was **your** mother!'*

I am not saying my mother-in-law is ugly, but she couldn't lure a bloke out of a burning house.

I am not saying that my mother-in-law is fat, but she puts her make up on with a paint roller.

I am not saying my mother-in-law is ugly, but when she appeared on television, they immediately put up a sign saying, *'Please Do Not Adjust Your Set.'*

I am not saying my mother-in-law is a big woman, but once, when she hung her knickers out on the line to dry, a family of gypsies turned up from nowhere and camped in them.

I am not saying my mother-in-law looks like a witch but she could resemble one if she tidied herself up a bit. In our neighbourhood, just to glance at her is regarded as a cure for hiccups.

I am not saying my mother-in-law has a large mouth, but when she smiles she gets lipstick on both her ears. She's the only person I know who can eat a banana sideways.

I am not saying my mother-in-law was an ugly baby, but for several weeks after she was born, they were putting the nappies on the wrong end.

My mother-in-law adores nature and that's really forgiving after what nature did to her.

I am not saying my mother-in-law is a bad cook, but in her house the mice bring their own sandwiches.

I am not saying my mother-in-law is fat but she does have bulges in places where other people don't even have places.

I hate my mother-in-law. Sure, I am well aware that if not for her, I wouldn't have my wife. And that's another reason I hate her.

I left my wife because of another woman – *her mother.*

Two cannibals were chatting over dinner. *'You know I hate my mother-in-law's guts,'* said one. *'Don't let it bother you,'* replied the other. *'Push them aside and eat your rice first.'*

My mother-in-law bought me two shirts for Christmas – a red one and a green one. On Christmas Eve I turned up in the dining room wearing the red shirt, just to please her. *''What's the matter with the green shirt?'* she snarled.

One morning my mother-in-law forgot to leave the garbage bin on the street for collection. When the garbage truck had just departed from the kerb, she ran after it shouting, *'Wait a moment please, or am I too late?'*

'No,' replied the driver. *'Just jump in, quickly.'*

My mother-in-law is a noisy eater. Last week at a restaurant, when she started on her soup, three couples got up and began to dance.

My mother-in-law has a slight speech impairment. Every so often she pauses to breathe.

And finally,

Speaking of mothers-in-law, generally speaking, my mother-in-law is generally speaking!

Julia Gillard (Born in 1961; Australia's Prime Minister 2010-2013)

Ending the book with a joke about MILS endlessly speaking just didn't feel right. Why not a real incessantly speaking person? And not just any person. Someone sophisticated as well and not only in appearance, but also progressive in thinking, in judgment and in formulating strategies and policies of vital importance to mankind.

Oops – I think *"mankind"* may not be politically correct. Should it be *womankind?* But what does womankind mean? It's apparently same as womanhood. That's as the other sex to manhood.

Checking the definition of manhood, one of its meanings is a "euphemism for a man's genitalia". It got me confused. What's feminism for a man's genitalia? Sorry, I didn't read it properly. It should read *euphemism* for … that. It looks that I am struggling with these terms.

Indeed, I find it very confusing. And further, if manhood is synonym for a man's ... you know what; does it mean that likewise, womanhood is the same as ... a woman's that?

No – I am told. I got it all wrong. It's not manhood and it's not womanhood. That's not right either. Let's start again. It's not mankind, nor womankind. It should be humankind.

It took a while to clarify that and I'm still not sure I got it right.

I am saying this because the above inference seemed logical. I'd gone before through a series of linguistic associations and came to the conclusion that humankind is no more than a big, collective ... that. Anything wrong with that?

Anyway, talking about sophisticated people, I mentioned earlier in the book that a certain Australian ex-Prime Ministers always exhibited a chic hairstyle. Here I am not implying that this ex was an ex-hibitionist.

If you don't recall who that person is, I will just say that I'll finish the book as I started it. With former Prime Minister, Ms Julia Gillard. That's last, but not least.

So, Julia was born in 1961, as Barry. No – Julia was born in the town of Barry. So, she was born in Wales, of Irish and Scottish ancestry. Hmm ...

In 1966 her parents migrated to Australia and settled in Adelaide. Regrettably, they brought Julia with them. It would have been so much simpler for everyone in this country if they hadn't.

So, Julia is not indigenous to Australia. Had she migrated to the United States, their Constitution wouldn't have allowed her to be President, which is such a shame. I mean it is a shame that our Constitution is not similar to that of the Yankees'.

In Adelaide Julia attended "Mitcham Demonstration School", which probably explains her future political affiliations. These left-oriented folks always whinge and protest and demonstrate.

Later she studied Farts and Law. Sorry – she studied *Arts and Law* and even worked as a lawyer specialising in Industrial Law. During her time as a lawyer with a reputable Melbourne-based firm, Julia caused plenty of hullabaloo. Actually thanks to Julia's scams, after she joined the practice, they rapidly became anything but reputable.

It was alleged that Julia and her boyfriend at the time set up a "slush fund" in the name of Australian Workers Union, from which they slashed a bob or two for private and personal minor use. Like the purchase of a house in Melbourne's upmarket suburb of Fitzroy.

Having become in 1983 only the second ever woman to lead the Australian Union of Students, in 1998 Julia entered federal politics winning the Labor seat of Lalor. But Julia was never happy to be second.

Interestingly given Julia's background, Lalor is a suburb of Melbourne and also an Irish surname meaning Half Leper. Why half … I don't know.

After entering politics, Julia's milestone coup happened in 2006 when she started dating hairstylist Timmy, who is best known for establishing the lucrative salon "Tim Mathieson

Pubic Hair", in Ship-Fart-On, Victoria. Sorry – I am told the suburb was *Shepparton* and *Pubic* was not included in the name of the business. It should have been – in my opinion.

In 2010 Julia was second in charge in the Labor Government and in the Party's ranks. She wanted to be first. So, this time, not just in an ordinary coup, but in a coup d'état, she amicably took what she thought should be rightly hers. That was the first job. The incumbent was Kevin Rudd.

Rudd's job at the time was Prime Minister of Australia. Having been unceremoniously dumped, he wept a little on national television but was otherwise affable with the changeover. Labor teammates of Julia assured her that everything was fine and dandy and she had nothing to feel guilty about. She didn't.

As Prime Minister, naturally, her pinnacle moment was her 2012 "misogyny speech" already talked about in this book. From there on, her fame went up and up, and ... finally ... in flames.

This is in short the remarkable career of an extraordinary Scot-Irish-Welsh-Aussie woman who, given her legendary ambition to succeed, could surely have become overseas something like Duchess of Cambridge or Princess of Denmark or whatever, but elected instead to become a pain in the back Down Under.

From my personal perspective I should be thankful to Ms. Gillard for delivering the misogyny speech because, if not for it, I wouldn't have put this book together.

Conclusion

I started this book by disapproving of Julia Gillard's misogyny speech and ended it by thanking Ms Gillard for (unwittingly) prompting me to write it. I mean the book, not the misogyny speech! They say the speech was written by a man but it wasn't me!

It was apparently a bloke named John McTernan – once Director of Communications and Media Adviser to the Australian Prime Minister. The Prime Minister was none other than Julia Gillard.

What an idiot! I mean this McTernan, not the Australia Prime Minister.

Anyway, no hard feelings. I will just add that I wish Ms Gillard good luck in whatever she has chosen to do after her time in politics.

I hear these days Ms Gillard is backing Hillary Clinton in her bid to become the next US President. Well, I suppose Julia could do worse than that. I mean she could support the other tramp. But … wait a minute. Did I just say tramp? A billionaire tramp? Probably not. Perhaps just trump. Donald Trump.

And we, Aussies could have done much worse than having Julia Gillard as PM for three years. I mean there is a good chance that the Yanks will get Trump for four years!

Talking about Trump, it is of interest to note that both male and female columnists at major media outlets have labeled him "a sexist dinosaur," with "a legacy of unapologetically gleeful misogyny."

Perhaps I should have dedicated a section in this book to him. But no! It would have been a waste of space and time.

Like Sigmund Freud – for example. I find him such a bore! Apparently he's a misogynist too! I actually did mention Freud briefly in the "Introduction", but maybe I should have cited one of his quotes which is relevant to the subject. It gives a good insight of his attitude towards the other gender.

"Despite my thirty years of research into the feminine soul, I have not yet been able to answer the great question that has never been answered: What does a woman want?" That's what Freud himself once said – as simple as that.

Well, my comment to that would be: Has Sigmund Freud ever found any answers to anything? Actually, Freud himself once said, "In the Middle Ages they would have burnt me. Now they are content with burning my books."

One of Freud's contemporaries was German-American journalist Henry Louis Menken. Though he was apparently famous, I probably wouldn't know of him if not for his very original definition of a misogynist. According to Mencken, a misogynist is "a man who hates women as much as women hate one another."

I wouldn't dare to add any comment to that!

But I will end the book with a joke, which, on the face of it, has nothing to do with the topics discussed. It has however a lot to do with the world we live in today. It's a mad, mad, mad, mad world, as they say and getting crazier by the day!

In a restaurant somewhere a man sits at a table and quietly sips from his coffee. He has no iPhone, no laptop, no iPad … He just sits there, like a psychopath.

Kings, Queens and the Sordid In-between
Stefan Raicu

ISBN: 9781925367591   **Qty:**   .....

RRP   AU $24.99

Postage within Australia   AU $5.00

TOTAL* $_____

* All prices include GST

Name:...

Address: ....

....

Phone: ....

Email: ....

Payment: ( ) Money Order ( ) Cheque ( ) MasterCard ( ) Visa ( )

Cardholder's Name:...

Credit Card Number: ....

Signature: ....

Expiry Date: ....

Allow 7 days for delivery.

Payment to: Marzocco Consultancy (ABN 14 067 257 390)
PO Box 12544
A'Beckett Street, Melbourne, 8006
Victoria, Australia
admin@brolgapublishing.com.au

BE PUBLISHED

Publish through a successful publisher.
Brolga Publishing is represented through:
• **National** book trade distribution, including sales,
marketing & distribution through **Macmillan Australia.**
• **International** book trade distribution to
    • The United Kingdom
    • North America
    • Sales representation in South East Asia
• **Worldwide e-Book distribution**

For details and inquiries, contact:
Brolga Publishing Pty Ltd
PO Box 12544
A'Beckett St VIC 8006

Phone: 0414 608 494
markzocchi@brolgapublishing.com.au
ABN: 46 063 962 443
(Email for a catalogue request)

www.ingramcontent.com/pod-product-compliance
Lightning Source LLC
Chambersburg PA
CBHW071423090426
42737CB00011B/1549